New Eyes

the human side of change leadership

Editors: Joanne Flinn, Roberto Saco,
Mike Staresinic, and Dan Ballbach

FastPrint
Publishing

www.fast-print.net/store.php

An environmentally friendly book printed and bound in England by
www.printondemand-worldwide.com

Mixed Sources

Product group from well-managed
forests, and other controlled sources

FSC www.fsc.org Cert no. TT-COC-002641
© 1996 Forest Stewardship Council

PEFC Certified

This product is
from sustainably
managed forests
and controlled
sources

PEFC www.pefc.org
PEFC/16-33-415

This book is made entirely of chain-of-custody materials

To those who toil in the fields of change

New Eyes: the human side of change leadership provides powerful concepts and practical examples to help organisations avoid the common pitfalls in trying to implement transformational change. The authors illustrate effective methods that engage the hearts and minds of employees to internalise the change that is necessary for letting go of the old and embracing the new.

Dr John C. Timmerman
Senior Strategist - Customer Experience and
Innovation, The Gallup Organisation

Leading big changes in global organisations is a journey - it's refreshing to read of the journey others have taken, to learn from them and to be given the space to reflect. New Eyes helps the change leadership conversation.

Maria Pathrose, Strategic Programs, HP-Shell

This is the first book I've read that successfully and interestingly integrates some of the most challenging areas of organisational change, interweaving theory and practice in an encouraging way. The authors share their success stories of managing sustainable change in an inspirational and contagious way. While especially relevant for OD practitioners and change leaders, everyone interested to develop change leadership will prosper from reading it. Get this book and be inspired to lead change!

Caroline Palmstedt
Regional Director, Asia
NeuroLeadership Institute

When we set up the Consulting and Coaching for Change Executive Programme, our aim was to offer a transformational experience for change agents.

The papers of this volume demonstrate that former participants have not only embarked on a life-long learning journey, but they truly act as reflective practitioners. Their inputs, based on their personal experience, are undoubtedly extremely relevant for everyone responsible for leading change.

Bertrand Moingeon
Professor and Deputy Dean of HEC Paris, co-
founder of the Consulting and Coaching for
Change Executive Program, jointly run by Oxford-
Said Business School and HEC Paris

The great value of this book is that it offers a number of open windows onto the worlds of change leaders in institutions and corporations. Faced with so many rapid developments in the availability and processing of information, in possibilities for networking and communication how are those responsible for organisational change thinking and talking and practicing? Here is the chance to listen in on practical and reflective practitioners with a wide range of experience as they describe, explore, propose and inquire into what works and how to work. This book allows readers to tap into what's happening in an evolving field.

Dr Patricia Shaw
Visiting Professor at the Business
School, Hertfordshire University, and Fellow of
Schumacher College for Sustainability Studies
(Devon, UK).
Author, "Changing Conversations in Organisations."

Leaders and managers have to face uncertainty within their organisations all the time. Making sense of change – for themselves, and for the people who depend on them – is therefore a critical skill.

Today, the creation of value requires leveraging the forces of transformation for lasting advantage. Which is why experienced practitioners from around the globe have always known that being "ahead" of change is better than being in its "wake". Yet, rapid technological and societal change in an interconnected world, ill prepares managers and business leaders on how to triumph, when conditions are in a perpetual state of evolution.

I'm delighted therefore, that the Change Leaders have brought out this elegant book, to add to a vital body of knowledge. As the title suggests, it recognises that change is about people and the creation of meaning, even within turbulence. I heartily recommend this insightful book to leaders everywhere.

Bharat Wakhlu
Resident Director, Tata Services (India).
Author, "Total Quality – Excellence through
Organisation-wide Transformation"

New Eyes is a welcome addition to a growing movement to grow an ecosystem of approaches to leadership in complex adaptive systems. The chapter entitled "Deviance, Discovery and Delight" by Lewis and Saco describes how an innovative approach called Positive Deviance (PD) prevents hospital acquired infections by liberating hidden solutions and occult change agents that already exist within healthcare facilities. The PD approach is also liberating and amplifying existing solutions to complex problems in mental health, education and our aging population.

Jon C. Lloyd, MD, Sr. Associate, Positive Deviance
Initiative

A decade ago, two great universities, Oxford and HEC, had an idea: join together and create an advanced degree programme focused on illuminating how modern organisations change. The first year of the programme lead to another idea: create The Change Leaders and this book is the latest example of its on-going contributions to the practice of organisational change. The insights of the accomplished practitioners and scholars found here on how real change happens in 21st century organisations are profoundly important and available nowhere else. New Eyes is a must have.

Walter McFarland
2013 Board Chair of the American Society for
Training and Development, Co-author "Choosing
Change"

Contents

New Conversations

Rafael Ramirez

My experience of the Coaching and Consulting for Change (CCC) programme offered jointly by Oxford and HEC since 2003 was first as a facilitator (or 'mid-wife') for this Joint Venture coming about. Then once it was agreed, working with the first co-directors, Elizabeth and Denis and several colleagues from both institutions in designing it; and with the next co-directors, Rachel and Marc in refreshing it. And since the beginning, teaching in it.

Most of the rather courageous participants attending the CCC programme over the years were 'reflective practitioners', as Donald Schön famously called such professionals. CCC articulated a different way of doing this reflective practice, one where the reflection-research and the pedagogic components became relatively more important than the practice one had been prior to their joining. Others and I urged participants to retain this new balance – to reflect and teach and learn (more) after graduation.

This book reflects efforts in this sense. It is a welcome manifestation on how enduring and enriching the rebalancing between reflection, pedagogy, and practice can be – also for practice.

It is reasonable to propose that thinking about 'change as acceleration' is a late twentieth century view. It is seen as a characteristic of change since CCC was started. Think for example of "competing against time" – an influential book by Stalk and Hout from BCG published in 1990. My own work on Turbulence with colleagues has added the idea that change is not only faster, but also more unpredictable.

Now we consider change agents face more messy or "wicked" situations (situations more than problems). In turbulence, old recipes and 'solutions' may not only be ineffective; but if deployed, can make the situation more difficult to understand and engage with. I explored this with Jerry Ravetz in our piece on "Feral Futures".

The scales (from global to very local, and in between) of change and their interconnections pose another interesting set of challenges. What one does 'here and now' may have terrible consequences 'there and then'; yet 'there and then' has no client (yet) or set of stakeholders with whom to engage in the here and now of actual change.

Media and communications technologies have redressed imbalances of information access. Facebook and Blackberry are alleged to have been important in Mubarak's downfall, a scenario that Newsweek tells us the US administration failed to imagine. And these technologies have made privacy an obsolete concept: even the head of the most powerful information agency in the world, the CIA, has had his (presumably presumed secret) personal life found out and was forced to resign. Interconnectivity may mean that it is more rational for someone living in Lima or in Luanda to be concerned about the valuation of the renminbi than about who gets elected to public office in their home town.

The world is possibly about to see the non-proliferation treaty become obsolete. Will a new nuclear war era be like Pakistan and India? Or is the scenario much more like what the hawks worry about with Iran and North Korea? And how will what we now consider "medicine" and "social care" look like when our grandchildren are our age? How will these grandchildren consider global warming? Will limited liability be revoked in time to avoid climate change becoming irreversible?[1]

So, what is to be done? The authors of this volume suggest we focus on our perspectives, in ways Proust first articulated: "The real voyage of discovery consists not in seeking new landscapes, but in having new eyes."

The Change Leaders is a ten-year-old community of change management practitioners with roots in Oxford and Paris – all graduated from the CCC programme. They've gone back to places of ancient learning to ascertain insights and possibilities for change in the work world. The Change Leaders as reflective practitioners seek to more or less comfortably straddle two domains that struggle to communicate with each other: academia and the "busy-ness" world. In academe, rigorous reflection is privileged; in the busy business world, it is action and results that matter most. Yet the lack of comfort can drive movement and inquiry, and in this case critical reflections on practice.

It is the authors' and editors' hope – and mine, the privileged preface writer – that the writings in this volume contribute to improve the quality of conversations. Perhaps even they will help start new conversations. The hope is that these in turn will spawn initiatives, guide or inform experiments and prototypes, identify new researchable topics. The effort of those that have contributed to this volume is commendable and I hope it leads to action that people and communities will with hindsight find significant.

Rafael Ramirez
Oxford
August 2013

Director of the Oxford Scenarios Programme and Fellow in Strategy at the Saïd Business School and Green Templeton College, University of Oxford. Rafael is one of the world's leading experts on scenario planning and a founder of theories on the aesthetics of business, work and organisation.

[1] Dangerman, J. A. T.C. and Schellnhuber, H.J. 2013. Energy systems transformation. Proceedings of the National Academy of Sciences of the USA. Published online before print January 7, doi: 10.1073/pnas.1219791110

Meaning Change

Art Kleiner

According to the dictionary I have at my fingertips – the Oxford English Dictionary in this case, but it could really be any good one – the word "change" doesn't mean what this book suggests it means. To an ordinary person, using words in an ordinary way, it means "the act of making or becoming different; an alteration or modification." Or, in its most commonly used day to day form, the act of taking off one article of clothing and putting on another. In daily life, the closest people come to change management is when they have to figure out how many pairs of pants to take into the dressing room.

But for readers of the book you have in your hand, "change" clearly means something more substantive. This is a book by, and for, change agents. It is put together by people who studied together at a programme of intervention and management wisdom, a programme which spans two great universities and a multitude of cultures, and which – by its nature – brings together a variety of fields, including economics, organisational studies, psychology, and sociology. Its goal is to help build a cadre of people who can help organisations solve the very real challenges facing them. "Change" is the problem, and also the remedy, and therefore the meaning of the word is crucial. So at the outset of this book, let's spend a little time together thinking about what people mean by "change."

As it happens, organisational change is one of two realms where "change" means something different than the dictionary definition. The other field is personal growth. In that field, which includes much (but not all) of clinical psychology and nearly all of addiction treatment, to "change" means to give up old bad habits and to take on a new, enlightened form of behaviour. Change of this sort is generally recognised as something easy to start but hard to maintain; the goal, paradoxically, is to make change last.

The idea of personal change is also noteworthy in that it tends to embody (against the wish of many of its practitioners) the idea of original sin. The practice of personal growth evokes the idea that many individual human beings are trapped in problematic states because they started out fallen. They do the bad things they do, as the singer Harry Nilsson once put it, "cause I done what I did when I was a kid" – or, at the very least, because of forces and influences that work below the level of consciousness. From the messy, miserable, addiction-ridden starting points that many individuals find themselves in, any change -- whether through secular or religious means – is assumed to be improvement.

Organisational change has yet a third definition, and it may not involve change at all. To be sure, a shift of identity is involved. Indeed, the word "transformation" is often used to emphasise how sweeping that transition is supposed to be. But underneath, organisation change is the process of bringing an organisation to a more ideal state – whether or not that involves a real shift of identity.

When organisational leaders say they want their organisation to transform, they're really expressing a wish to preside over a productive, high-performing enterprise. This state of virtue may be difficult to realise, but we all know what it would feel like, in our heart of hearts. It would be a thriving, intrinsically collaborative and rewarding place enterprise, where people work hard and get results, but don't waste time with busy work. It should be socially and environmentally responsible. It should make enough money to reward its members and stakeholders commensurate with their expectations. (If they're ambitious senior leaders this may require a lot of profit.) It should attract a group of people so engaged and mutually supporting that other great people are drawn to work with them. But no one should be required to stay at work a moment longer than necessary, so they can still have time for a rewarding private life. This is the kind of place where engineers and marketers go out for drinks together to gossip about the customers, and where the combination of skills – analytic and verbal, professional and amateur, specialised and whole-person, novice and experienced, taught and learned, tacit and explicit – contributed by different members of the team leads to a result that is greater than the sum of its parts. Someone once told me that Toyota designed its U.S. assembly plants with the idea that people should come off an 8-hour shift energised and satisfied, like they'd just left a health club after a bracing workout. That's what the end of a day at a post-change organisation should feel like.

How do you get there from here? That's the question that organisation change efforts seek to answer. Many leaders – and the interveners they work with – seem to believe that the more profound and sharp the change involved, the more likely they are to reach the goal. But in many cases, the goal is actually pretty close to where the organisation started, and it still has many of those qualities. If it weren't for all those people who came in for the money and power, mucking about with their carping and backstabbing, then maybe it would still be in that state of grace, with all the charm of the small backyard workshop, garage, homespun lab or graduate school classroom where it was conceived. Meanwhile, many leaders are so focused on getting rid of all the snags and pain points that they forget that the original virtues are still there. They forget why they were attracted to this organisation in the first place.

In short, I'm suggesting that the word "change" might be a misnomer for the real subject of this book: the progress of organisations to a generally better place. In the spirit of being careful what you wish for, serious change may be the opposite of what the organisation truly needs. The leader may really want to have an organisation that is more like the best of itself, and not really changed at all.

This fits more closely with the way human society was organised for millennia. Before the industrial revolution, organisations were expected to improve slowly. Most people grew up expecting to live all their lives in a locked-in society, unaware of alternatives. Even entrepreneurs were stable souls, members of great lineages of traders and merchants. They spent their lives fulfilling business relationships that had been forged generations before; they married deliberately to ensure that their family-owned enterprises would continue. Change was not a cure for organisational problems; it was a disease.

But if change isn't really change, then organisational interveners face a dilemma. They are expected to produce a genuine transformation, but they're most effective if they help a company get closer to its identity. They're also working with people who evolved their organisational senses through millennia of stability. Not only that. The principles by which change occurs are untested, unpredictable, obscure, and often mutually contradictory.

They are hired under a variety of named purposes, but they are usually asked the same thing: to align the formal structures – codes of conduct, written rules, reporting relationships, and so on – with the unwritten knowledge and behaviour that comprises an organisation's culture. In other words, they have to bring change to the rigid, while celebrating the stability and identity of the evanescent. To accomplish this, they use a variety of techniques which you will read about in this volume: writing, workshops, scenarios, playgrounds for adults, and so on. They propose a variety of organisational redesign moves, including abandoning hierarchies in favour of workflows, and codifying ethics and externalities.

The result is a book of theories of organisational change – with the third definition: the progress of organisations toward a generally better place. We may never reach a time of perfect consensus of what a better place means, or how one should get there. And the theories in this book are far from uniform. But organisational change should not be treated as a science. It is an emerging craft, with true mastery attainable by those who practice. Here are the starting points.

Art Kleiner
New York
August 2013

Art Kleiner is editor-in-chief of *strategy+business*, the award-winning management magazine published quarterly in print and weekly online by Booz & Company. He is the author of *The Age of Heretics* and *Who Really Matters: The Core Group Theory of Power, Privilege, and Success*. Formerly, he was the editorial director of Peter Senge's *Fifth Discipline Fieldbook* series and an editor at the *Whole Earth Catalogue*.

New Eyes

From practice and reflection

We began this book wishing to help fellow leaders of change, change management and OD practitioners. In fact, we hope that anyone with more than a passing interest in sustainable change in organisations of all stripes might find this useful.

Change is one of those fluid things. We also found creating this book was fluid too. We decided it would be appropriate and beneficial to build a navigator for the unwary reader.

The set of articles in this volume reflects a major tenet of our training as change practitioners - the notion of multiple lenses by which to understand the world of change. There is no one best way to view change in a complex and diverse world, so by adopting many eyes, metaphors, tools and methods we get closer and more effective in an ever morphing reality.

Change Leaders were prepared to show up and explore what they'd seen work, research they'd done and practical tools to help change leaders. We selected eight for this volume. Some chapters explore new trends effecting change. Others explore more familiar territory from the lens of practice.

These articles are characterised by diversity, in content and point of view. There is logic, however, encompassing four sections: personal change, organisations and change, the greater societal context, and finally strategies for effecting and sustaining change.

Personal change

Society at large and the organisations coping within them are indeed changing rapidly. In this section, two articles describe effective ways in which action can support the personal journey in organisational change.

The most personal journey can be one of values and ethics. Margareta Barchan and Jeanne Westervelt Rice begin this volume with two approaches they have found useful and effective in influencing organisational and personal values. They discuss reflective practices in the work place, namely guided dialogues and reflective writing. How can we maintain or build upon a culture of integrity and ethics when so many things are changing around us? If change is constant, what remains? Using examples from their practice, Margareta and Jeanne address, for example, the inadequacy of Codes of Conduct in promoting ethical behaviour. They show us how structured approaches for reflection augment the probability of success in a more insightful application of standard approaches used in change focused at human behaviour and values.

Sometimes the best strategy a change agent or leader has at their disposal is going to back to basics; basics here, in the sense of appropriate – clear, consistent, and credible – communications when it comes to changing heads, hearts and hands. Susan Goldsworthy takes a fresh look at communications and leadership, reminding us of this powerful tool and its effective use by leaders. She enlists social psychology and motivational theory to offer suggestions for more effective change communications. As the purpose of communications is all important, we may also make better decisions with the sensible use of technology, particularly when a conversation can be just as or more effective than the most sophisticated devices.

Organisations and change

We've heard of the Velcro organisation, the boundary-less organisation, the flexible or adaptive nature of organisation, and even morphing organisations. Another couple of articles describe how organisations may respond to change.

The organisation of the future is considered by Silke Grotegut, Anja Reitz, and Wulf Schönberg. They call it Organisation 3.0. Focusing on large companies, they point to multi-generational sharing of work processes, the increasing role of personal values, longer and healthier life spans, the ubiquity of work, the growing impact of social media, and the nature of employee empowerment. They survey a variety organisational designs to build on the work of Niels

Pfläging, describe their journey into network organisations and describe organisational responses to these issues.

Long term sustainable business performance is a theme addressed by Martin Thomas. Using scenarios, he projects out to 2050 to look back on what leading organisations would do today. Given the nature of the environmental context, Martin proposes to use Purposeful Self-Renewing Organisations as a construct for a re-assessment for performance measurement systems in corporate governance. Are we measuring the right things in the right way? Is context adequately considered for the implications of 2050? Applying the concepts of triple bottom line, sufficiency, and sustainability Martin makes a case for an overhaul of our business measurement systems over the next decades.

The greater societal context

From the individual coping with change to organisational response, now to the greater society and some of the macro-trends that are driving change. How does technology simultaneously meet our needs as consumers and influence our perception of those very same needs? Are our minds capable of responding to the onslaught of technological change?

Big Data and its broad impact in our lives including in our work lives as leaders and managers is considered by Mick Yates. He emphasises the need for leaders to prepare their organisations particularly in this era of unprecedented and rapid informational change. Mick discusses ways in which Big Data interacts and blends with concepts like customer centricity and innovation networks. Finally, he introduces a pragmatic leadership framework for enabling organisational performance.

If technology is changing our outer world, is it changing our inner world? John O'Loan sees digital technology is not only changing the exterior nature of reality but also our interior landscape, our brains and minds. In an age of hypertext and cut-and-paste, we process information differently and hence think differently. John brings to bear on this topic the work of Walter Ong, Dan Tapscott, and particularly Jason Lanier. The latter has become a leading proponent of 'lock-in' where we become conditioned to think in set patterns. Our highly advanced technology, software, and algorithms can assume the role of strait jackets in society. John points to a change.

Strategies for effecting and sustaining change

We explore the nature of special problems in change management. Thus, we end the volume with our prime concern and turn back to organisations in the midst of change. Apparently logical problems of process and policy may be technically a wicked problem about human behaviour.

Joanne Flinn and Alexander Budzier look at two key entities in the changing world of work: Board of Directors and project teams. The former still wield significant power over policy and increasingly execution. Project teams form the means for which work actually gets done in many industries today. Regulatory pressures place additional demands on Board governance. The very nature of wicked problems require a different mind-set to change. Joanne and Alexander explore the nature of risk in project-based work and how the risk misperceived or ignored by Boards, is at their own peril. They provide practical actions for Boards and Project Teams to reduce risk (and improve value) using muddy management.

Finally, Jane Lewis and Roberto Saco tackle one of the most surprising and unusual change management movements of the past 15 years, Positive Deviance, also called the Bright Spots approach to change. With personal insights garnered from proximity to Jerry and Monique Sternin, the developers or founders of this approach, and many other practitioners, Jane and Roberto delve into the nitty-gritty of work in the field, mainly in the UK where Jane has her practice. They also address the wider aspects of fit within the landscape of change management methods and philosophies.

All the best with Change!

The Editors

Joanne Flinn, Roberto Saco, Mike Staresinic, and Dan Ballbach

The Road to

Redemption

How to reclaim a corporate culture

of integrity

Margareta Barchan and
Jeanne Westervelt Rice

The CEO of a large European-based construction company picked up the newspaper one morning and was startled to read negative headlines about his closest competitors. The article cited back-room deals, material losses left off the books, and other shady accounting and business practices. He was struck by the thought that his company was lucky that it was not also named in the article. Deception and dishonesty were routine in that industry. Even customers came to accept and expect it.

This CEO chose to heed the wake-up call. Recognising that the stock value of this publicly traded company, the brand value, and many jobs—including his own—were at risk, he decided to do something to change the company's culture. Because culture is deeply rooted in every aspect of any business, the decision to make such wide-scale, values-based change was not quick or easy.

Committing to culture change at the values-based level takes guts, and it's not something that happens every day. Even when shareholders demand more transparency and mass media cries foul, those at the helm during some of the world's largest corporate scandals pass the buck and refuse to accept responsibility—at least not full responsibility. Why? Because even when they are caught red-handed, it is much easier to pay the fines and wait out the media storm than it is to change ingrained corporate culture.

At least that used to be true. We believe a "perfect storm" that could sweep in an era of sustainable change is taking shape. First, government regulation is on the rise, and if not creating mass change, it's at least making inroads to tidy up very loose ends. Second, a new breed of business leader is coming of age and these professionals cut their teeth in a global business arena in a world plagued by environmental issues. Third, evolving research into human organisational development and a host of new communication and education tools make it easier and quicker to communicate with the masses.

As we have spent most of our professional careers as managers, directors and consultants in Europe and the USA, we have experienced both successful and less successful ways of leading companies. This chapter is on the new edge, we are excited by it as we see it working. Our recent work in the field of business operational strategy and strategic communication has been focused on the challenge facing many of our clients: how to create a culture of professional integrity, and how to implement sustainable business practices. Integrity is a prerequisite for a lasting business.

In this article, we present the findings of our own study around workplace ethics, we describe the missing element of reflection as a critical component in developing mindful leaders, we introduce new applications for two standard communication tools (talking and writing), and we present a short-list of our best practices for creating an atmosphere of trust and integrity in any workplace.

When Good Employees Choose Wrong

The road to ethical business practices is paved with good intentions. Compliance officers are hired. Educational programmes are purchased. New employees are versed in the values, codes, and regulations that drive the business. Still, we are surprised—and sometimes caught red-handed—when global market conditions change and leave us feeling raw and exposed.

What was legal yesterday is not today; what was once socially acceptable is now taboo. One company's traditions and values are usurped by another's in a merger or takeover. The more we try to keep up, the more complex our task becomes. Ask anyone in compliance, human resources, or corporate communications: the pace is unsustainable, the task too cumbersome.

Despite our best efforts to create and communicate the values, codes, and regulations that mean good business, misconduct happens. Sometimes people simply choose to do wrong, and we all know that it takes only one high profile case of malfeasance to wreak havoc resulting in losses in the millions or billions in terms of jobs and money.

We are not here to belabour the obvious. To create the foundation of a corporate culture that breeds right action, you must communicate codes, values, and regulations clearly and consistently. You must establish consequences for misbehaviour, and the rules must apply to everyone equally, regardless of position, tenure, or personal relationships. A transparent and value based organisation is more likely to create commitment and motivation in our experience. (See Martin Thomas on the implication of increasing transparency thanks to social media and Mick Yates on Big Data).

Even with these safeguards in place, and big budgets invested in ethics training, people continue to rationalise their own misconduct in the workplace, turn a blind eye to the misdemeanours of their colleagues and business partners, and fail to take the right action on a daily and consistent basis.

The problem is right action in the workplace doesn't seem to happen *naturally*. But it can, and it should.

Assuming the values, rules, and regulations have been communicated, the challenge is how to get employees to make the leap from knowing about them to living them—applying them consistently in the course of their daily jobs as right action behaviours.

Published values do not seem to have much impact on the workforce. In January 2013, we issued an online survey ("Workplace Ethics")[1] asking several hundred business professionals around the world six questions about ethics and values in the workplace. 125 responded. In one open-ended question, we asked them to tell us why, to the best of their knowledge, someone had violated a published rule or regulation. After lack of awareness and understanding (65%), stress or pressure to perform were the most frequent responses among the group. It seems that speed is more important than how things are done. Values are not the core of business practice for many companies.

Other key findings suggested by our survey indicate that most employees do not feel aligned with their company's published code of ethics (66%), that companies do not provide enough opportunities for the workforce to make personal connections to the regulations (60%), and, in a final, open-ended question about a company's biggest challenge to workplace integrity, several respondents stated that "management does not lead by example," and a few others indicated that management views themselves as "above the law."

Prioritisation is an idea we extrapolated from the survey answers, (but was not specifically asked about). It seems that most of our respondents were educated on codes of conduct and workplace values only when they joined as a new employee. Yet many respondents noted that there was no further training, or as one professional put it, "no reminders," which leads us to believe that there is not enough time or attention focused on ethical practices in

The Rule Breakers

A few candid comments from 125 business professionals around the world on why someone might violate a published rule or regulation:
- Insufficient real ownership of common values
- Senior management doesn't verify if everyone understands what is expected
- Personal and organisational values do not match
- Misunderstanding
- Cultural issues and differences
- Personal interests are valued more
- What's permitted is promoted

the course of daily activities. When asked off the record why, one vice president of a publicly held U.S. company said, "I have my own ethics. My personal standards are higher than the company's."

Imagine if most people thought this to be true. Of course, then, published codes would be viewed as guideposts for the organisation and not for the individuals.

Trying to keep up with ever-changing laws and regulations can be another challenge. "In some cases, I find that the code is no longer relevant to current circumstances," said one survey respondent. This is no surprise, as our own research into publicly available codes of conduct turned up detailed and complex documents that would, at best, serve as a reference guide, but would not be effective in guiding daily right action behaviours.

The Importance of Reflection

After a combined 50-plus years of coaching and consulting with business leaders in the areas of corporate social responsibility, sustainability, communication, and business development, we believe that it is possible to improve critical, ethical thinking on the job. We express this as "When you are seen, it becomes more important how you are seen."

The key is to help people reconnect to *people*. It's easier to lie, cheat, steal, cut corners, or bend the rules when a faceless organisation takes the hit. It's easier to justify or rationalise our misbehaviour when we think of it as a victimless crime. It is quite another when we consider the potential impact of wrongdoing on our colleagues, friends, and business partners who may lose jobs, homes, life savings, and more. To connect the impact of our actions to other *people* requires time for reflection.

Best practices in adult learning indicate that people make behavioural changes only when they have had the chance to process or internalise new information for themselves. In his book *The Power of Learning: Fostering Employee Growth*[2], learning design guru Klas Mellander describes a five-step adult learning process that makes important distinctions between "training" and "learning." It is one thing to train a workforce about codes of conduct or company values; it is quite another to know that the workforce has internalised or "learned" the information contained within. The difference, Mellander writes, is that in true learning, "information is converted into experience and insight."[2] In other words, once it is learned, it is very difficult to unlearn, like riding a bike.

Over the years, we have come to rely on and trust two learning tools that are essential in providing time for reflection—a process that helps people first become aware of, then process and internalise, and finally apply naturally new skills or knowledge. These two tools are: 1) guided dialogues – the exchange of information and ideas through facilitated discussions; and 2) reflective writing techniques – short, structured writing experiences that provide an opportunity to think critically and process our own behaviours, beliefs, and values.

We used these tools in our recent leadership development practices and collected anecdotal feedback supporting their effectiveness. We've seen that guided dialogues and reflective writing have a positive impact on three main challenges facing any organisation or leadership looking to create, foster, or ensure a culture of integrity:

1. Robust training, which results in real learning (internalisation);
2. Personalisation, which helps employees connect written codes and policies directly to people and the everyday aspects of their jobs, thus reducing the phenomenon of "victimless crimes";
3. Consistency, which means that the codes, policies, and values apply equally to everyone in an organisation, from top to bottom, with no exception.

We will demonstrate the effectiveness and efficiency of these two robust communication tools in these three areas, first separately and then together, drawing on our own experience and observations in the field, client feedback, and current research and findings.

Dialogues for Change

The construction company's CEO liked the outline of an ethics-based workshop that could be rolled out to the entire organisation. Working with his top leadership team, he incorporated company specific and proprietary information into the discussion.

Not a single employee in the company was left out. In the workshop setting, small groups of employees were presented with a number of difficult situations, taken from their on-the-job experiences, including customers demanding cash pay-offs, illegal dumping activities, and colleagues looking to cut corners to save time or reduce their workload. The participants were guided through a structured dialogue process and asked to use the published code of conduct to determine if violations had occurred, to what degree, and how to handle them. Legal representatives were on hand to clarify regulatory issues and offer guidance in grey areas. The programme also engaged colleagues in success stories, that is, times when someone broke with tradition and refused to compromise values, their own or the company's, to the benefit of all concerned.

Content was drawn directly from the company's codes and value statements to frame the guided dialogues and create meaningful exchanges. Various interpretations of these guidelines were presented to small groups of participants, who then shared reactions and discussed how the situations would realistically be handled on the job.

Guided dialogues are an effective way to help people consider their own personal values, to align these values with the organisation's, and reflect on their own behaviours in different situations, past and future. In this situation, participants were often surprised to discover that while they *said* they supported a published code, the actions they took on the job, which were ingrained and routine, indicated the opposite. There was a clear disconnect between spoken values and on-the-job behaviours.

One year after the dialogue-based programme rolled out, the company reported a significant reduction in violations on the job, and senior management continued to clarify policies to help employees handle ambiguous situations. To date, the CEO has successfully protected his company from negative publicity by turning the corporate culture around.

In Scandinavia, the founder of an alliance is driven by passion, energy, and integrity. Building this rapidly growing organisation with streamlined fulltime staff, but serving the interests of 3,000 companies representing about 200,000 employees, he identified seven core values which reflect his own entrepreneurial beliefs and ideals. As he is actively engaged in the daily business, one would expect a high level of compliance with the values, but employee actions indicated otherwise. With some preliminary research on our part, the crux of the problem became apparent very quickly, that is the employees did not recognise the importance attributed to values by the business owner, and that the values were open to a wide range of personal interpretation.

Speaking of Values...

Corporate values tend to leave a lot of room for individual interpretations – if not being more or less dismissed because of their paradoxical nature. One way to come to grips with this phenomenon is to provoke discussions, enabling people to reflect on what it means to actually live the values, and to take a stand. This also allows for people to ponder over what they as individuals truly stand for – in itself a desired achievement.

Provocative and contradictive statements, based on observed differences in views and behaviour, may do the trick. As in this example: *"For each 'value card', which side of the card describes best how we live/should live our values – A or B?"*

To align around the spirit of the values, we worked closely with the founder to create an engaging half-day workshop. We produced cards for each of the seven values; creativity, courage, diversity, responsibility, lifelong learning, endurance and customer focus. Each card was printed on two sides. One side indicated agreement and alignment with the value within the company; the other indicated that there was room for improvement or realignment was needed.

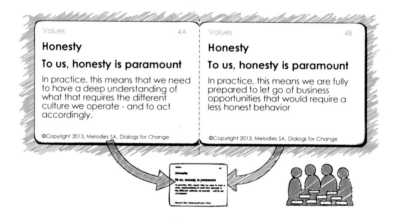

Figure 1: Example of a Dialogue Card

Working together in several small groups, the employees considered the statements on each side of the card and had to reach agreement on which side to place face-up on the table as their final answer. Discussions ensued. Arguments were made. Different opinions were considered. The conversations were lively, and the participants were actively engaged.

At the end of the round, each team shared its final decision about each value. Each team had to argue for their opinion on any value for which there was not consensus. In the course of the discussion, it became apparent that everyone cared about the values and were eager to work together and listen to different opinions, to align themselves on each value statement.

The final step pulled it all together. Values that did not align required clearer definitions and guidelines about on-the-job application. The participants worked together with the company founder to develop a list of activities and action steps, and each of these was assigned to someone who would take responsibility for their development.

For this client, the most important outcome was a shared sense that the values (not all directly related to ethical behaviours) were not being honoured, that specific action steps were needed to bring about alignment, and that the discussions would continue.

Although it is too soon to measure the long-term impact or change in human behaviour for this client, organisational processes have been put in place and structural changes are being made. One senior-level leader was asked to resign because her personal beliefs were not aligned with the company's or with the rest of the leadership team's. Simply by putting a new framework in place, there will be continued gradual transformation in the way their business is done, and who is doing it.

Guided dialogues help people reflect on the meaning of values, codes, and regulations, and facilitate how these are applied in people's daily activities, thus not only making employees more aware of them, but also institutionalising a process by which to internalise them. These dialogues have the added benefit of giving people a voice, respecting their opinions, and helping them consider company values in alignment with their own beliefs.

Any organisation that provides opportunities for individuals to reflect and assign personal meaning to the standards will be rewarded with an energy that builds esprit de corps and more people working in alignment, with more integrity. Creating awareness at the organisational level may help those responsible for hiring to seek better-aligned candidates. In situations where individuals, upon reflection, determine that they are not aligned with the organisation's codes or values, they may choose to leave their job.

The "Write Way" to Right Action

The facilitator read aloud a value statement directly from the global company's employee handbook: "We are honest, trustworthy and accountable for our actions." A moment later, as instructed, a senior vice president looked into a mirror as the facilitator asked, "How does the person you see in the mirror reflect that value?" This is the most literal form of reflection. The experience is followed by a short, timed, and structured writing exercise.

In our experience, this writing activity consistently ranks highest among participants for its ability to increase *awareness* of the value or code, shift *perspective*, and to *think more critically* about decisions and actions related to the value or code on the job.

Generally speaking, when organisations publish their core values and codes of conduct, they are aiming to ensure right action universally. Although these values, codes, and regulations can be complex (50 pages or more is not unheard of in the accounting industry) those responsible for compliance really want a workforce they can trust, and a community of people acting with integrity, naturally, in every situation and even under intense pressure. Reflective writing may hold the key to establishing a connection between personal values and corporate values; and when that occurs, people will more naturally "do the right thing."

Reflective writing, also called intuitive writing or expressive writing, developed a following in the mid-1980s within the health and wellness community for its ability to help people recover from trauma. Seminal studies by James W. Pennebaker, a professor of psychology at the University of Texas at Austin, scientifically demonstrated biological (immune system), psychological (mood), and behavioural (performance) effects using short, guided writing techniques for as little as 20 minutes a day and for as few as four days in a row[3]. Later studies indicate that even five or 10 minutes of writing may yield measurable benefits.

Reflective writing may be slow to gain foothold in the corporate arena simply because the writing itself is personal and is not meant to be shared. The inherent value to the writer is in its safety—he or she is free to be completely honest and explore deeply rooted beliefs and values without fear of judgment or retribution. In the United States, we are just starting to see reflective writing, sometimes in the form of journaling, on the menu of services in progressive corporate wellness programmes.

Consider then the potential power of reflective writing in helping people shift their thinking, or connect more personally and more deeply, to matters of compliance and issues of integrity.

Inroads are already being made. In 2008, Cynthia Roberts, an associate professor with Purdue University, discusses in detail the importance of reflection in developing future leaders—her students. Roberts writes:

> Although professionals may have learned a body of knowledge and pattern of practice, it may be difficult to apply them in unique, complex or uncertain situations. Continuous learning in practice occurs through reflection-in-action (thinking on one's feet) as well as reflection-on-action (thinking upon completion of a project or particular activity).[4]

While the idea of reflection is not new to most experienced business leaders (especially if they are successful), the idea of reflective *writing* may be. Corporate educators and others responsible for ethics education are clearly searching for effective "how-to's." We know from experience that lecture-based programmes are rooted in passivity. We know that check-the-box software programmes may increase awareness but do little, if anything, to develop critical thinking skills or internalisation. But we are seeing, in practice, that case-based dialogues and written reflections change emotions and behaviours. Scientific research in the health and wellness arena,[5] along with strong anecdotal evidence in the business sector, supports this assertion.

Consider the following technique adapted from the work of Kathleen Adams[6], a gifted psychotherapist and thought leader in the field of expressive writing. The facilitator begins by reading a specific rule, such as "It is against the law to engage in insider trading," and includes any action-related details. The participants are then asked to individually brainstorm 100 ways in which breaking this rule would negatively impact any other person inside or outside the organisation. They reread and reflect on this experience using a structured analysis form. This activity provides an opportunity for the participants to draw a direct connection between unethical actions and the "victims" of the action, who now take the form of colleagues, friends, partners, family, and other loved ones. The inappropriate action is no longer aimed at a "faceless organisation" or perceived as a "victimless crime."

Feedback from business leaders is compelling. "I've always found that training and educational programmes that give me time to self-reflect have the most impact on my assessment of my own leadership style and value system," remarked one financial services executive. Other comments indicate that writing experiences like these remove the mental barrier that "This could never happen to me," and push their thinking deeper, considering ramifications if it were to happen to them. "I found this [reflective writing] to be very effective in helping me consider the impact of my actions and decisions on the job. Much more so than the [expletive] ethics training programmes that we typically go through," said the senior official of an international accounting firm, after a workshop. While these comments are heartening, they do not guarantee that behaviours will change. What does suggest future compliance, and even personal transformation, is what we already know about the human learning process, summarised earlier in Klas Mellander's work: once something is fully learned and internalised, it is not easily forgotten.

The studies by Pennebaker already proved that reflective writing, even for as little as 10 minutes, reduces stress. If it is true, then, that some people make poor choices (or wrong choices) because they are under intense stress or pressure on the job—as indicated by our own survey—taking a moment to try a reflective writing technique may become an effective equivalent of the old "counting to 10" before taking action. Reflective writing in the workplace is in its infancy, but anecdotal results are impressive, so the studies will not be far behind.

Raising the Bar on Compliance

Nothing can be done for companies and industries that are happy enough to "comply." Some organisations and business leaders choose and are content to "check the box" so regulators are satisfied, or they are legally protected in a court of law. A plethora of online compliance programmes, or efficient – but not effective beyond creating awareness - lecture-based courses suffice for their needs. However for business leaders vested in building a foundation of trust, respect, and integrity, we offer two ways to effectively raise the bar on compliance, and bring about a deeper understanding of company values, so employees may operate more naturally with more integrity on the job.

In our survey on workplace ethics, we asked this question:

> In providing education on codes of conduct, did your company or organisation provide opportunities to draw connections to your own personal values and beliefs?

The majority of respondents, nearly 60 percent, said they did not, and in comments, suggested that the opportunity to do so would be important. "If you want to bring about a real culture swing, you have to get people to connect to the rules in a personal and meaningful way," commented one survey respondent.

We believe that a "personal and meaningful way" is achieved through professionally guided dialogues and facilitated reflective writing experiences. Together, they are proving to be a powerful combination. We are not alone in this assumption.

Those Who Cares

An effective ethics developmental program answers these questions:

- Is it experiential?
- Is it practical?
- Does it respect the individual?
- Is there personal reflection and self-analysis?
- Does it reflect the real behaviour rather than the espoused values?

"Although one typically thinks of reflection in terms of the assignment of written exercises, such as journaling, it may be helpful to include other activities that provide alternative routes for sharing experiences and insights," writes Professor Roberts. "Discussion in class and between teammates can introduce students to alternative viewpoints, to challenge them to think critically and develop collaborative reflective skills necessary for participation in learning organisations."[7]

We concur with Roberts in her clear charge to those responsible for leadership education, and we would add, to those responsible for organisational compliance:

> As leaders are faced with an environment that grows increasingly complex, multicultural, and ambiguous, we are seeing an increasing focus on the value of reflective capacity as a means for meeting the challenge. Leadership is learning—at both the individual and group levels. The ability to reflect, however, is not necessarily an inherent attribute, but it must be cultivated over time, and unless one is actively engaged in the practice of reflection, it is doubtful that this capability will develop on its own.[8]

Integrity in the Workplace

It is worth stating the record that we do not believe that our guided dialogue and reflective writing programme will ever change the mind or behaviour of those scoundrels, villains, or thieves who set out with intention to line their pockets at the expense of others. We're not likely to be able to help anyone hard-wired to choose wrong.

We've seen our programmes create heightened awareness about existing codes, values, and accepted forms of behaviour in the workplace. We've seen people draw their own connections between a written code and their daily activities on the job. We've heard people say that they now understand the implications and ramifications of a violation on other *people*. Our clients have told us that they appreciate the opportunity to link corporate rules and regulations to their own personal values and beliefs—creating an alignment that enables them to make the right decisions more naturally, or at least to choose more mindfully.

To conclude, we'd like to share a few final thoughts and best practices that we've learned from our individual and shared experiences using guided dialogues and reflective writing to foster right action in the workplace.

A Dynamic Duo. Separately, guided dialogues and reflective writing techniques are an effective component of any ethics education or corporate social responsibility programme. Together, they harmonise the organisation's core values with personal beliefs and bring into balance and awareness the choices we make and why we make them. It's a powerful combination that brings more depth to awareness of published codes in a short period of time.

Once is not enough. Ethics training is often required for new hires. But if that's the only time the codes, values, or regulations are referred to, it's not enough. The programmes should be offered as part of any leadership development programme, routinely as a component of performance reviews, and most importantly, communicated and integrated into the daily business activities.

Leaders First. We are often asked if C-level executives, directors, managers, or business owners should participate in the sessions with the rest of the workforce. Whether they participate with others or separately in their own group depends on your corporate culture. If it is already inclusive and collaborative and there is no fear of retribution, by all means, mix the groups. If leadership presence would inhibit the process, then run them separately. What is most important is that leaders participate in the programme. Often, it is best if they go first.

Walk the talk. We contend that companies with the highest levels of integrity—which to us appear as creative, inspirational and productive—are those where organisational and individual values are aligned. This means that those in hiring positions must be aware of the values given priority in the organisation so they can make successful personnel decisions. It also means that individuals, who upon reflection (or other types of communication, such as continually being passed over for promotions) realise that they are not a good match for the company and resign. Leadership needs to support a longer, and possibly more expensive, hiring search and understand that when talent leaves, it may offer a better hiring opportunity.

Business leaders, and in fact even shareholders or owners, who are serious about creating a corporate culture based on ethics, and integrity, must demand that codes, values, and regulations be given more than lip service. We were surprised to find that only 17 percent of our survey respondents believe that there is "total trust" among their colleagues, and when we asked them to comment further, their responses had similar threads: "The codes of conduct are just cosmetics," wrote one. "Trust comes from the leadership, not from the codes," wrote another.

If you're serious about rebuilding an ethical and value-driven culture, consider the education programmes you currently have in place, and evaluate them against your expectations. Keep this in mind: individuals who personally identify with the codes, accept them as being in line with their own core values and beliefs, and who have had a chance to internalise them, will ultimately make the leap from awareness to action.

Mobilising Heads, Hearts and Hands

Communicating in Times of Change

Susan Goldsworthy

Communicating to Hearts

"Without credible communication, and lots of it, people's hearts and minds are never captured."
John Kotter

Communication is one of the most powerful and yet underappreciated tools that a change agent can employ in helping organisations to implement successful change.

In my role as an executive coach, change and communications consultant, as well as in my corporate VP role, Communications at Tetra Pak, I have seen many senior executives who are brilliant engineers, scientists, or analysts stumble when it comes to leading effective change communication. Their tendency is to focus only on the facts, to *inform* people about the change, in a top-down approach, ignoring the need to *inspire* and *involve* people. Sadly, communications efforts are all too often treated as an afterthought or taken for granted as leaders forget about its necessity and power within any change effort.

Executives and change leaders benefit from reflecting upon and being reminded of the strategic value of continuously assessing, retooling and adapting communication efforts in order to achieve desired results.

It is a tragedy that so much time is spent working on the 'what and why' of a change, and so little time is spent on the how and why of leading the change. In tough economic environments, it is more important than ever for change agents to champion the use of clear, consistent, and credible communication to engage employees. In this volatile and uncertain world, many people are nervous or uncertain about their future. In the absence of regular information, people tend to fill the void with F.U.D. (Fear, Uncertainty, and Doubt).

The latest neuroscience shows that when people feel they are under threat, they become more distant, closed, and problem-focused.[1] So at a time when a collaborative, motivated solutions approach is most required, creativity and innovation are stifled.

Sadly, the role of effective communication in the change journey is often appreciated only after a failed change effort. Too often, communication is an afterthought rather than a strategic tool that can make the difference between the 'make or break' of change.

Rather than just 'going through the motions' of communications, it is vital to understand the science and art of change communications.

Many changes require behavioural change. Achieving behavioural change requires on-going participative stakeholder engagement. David Snowden, former head of Knowledge Management at IBM, points out:

> Consider what happens in an organisation when a rumour of reorganisation surfaces: the complex human system starts to mutate and change in unfathomable ways; new patterns form in anticipation of the event. On the other hand, if you walk up to an aircraft with a box of tools in your hand, nothing changes.[2]

Indeed, research estimates that up to 75 percent of organisational change initiatives fail or do not achieve the promised results.[3]

What is real

So what's happening? Why does change cause so much anxiety, stress, and negative emotion? As a real-life practitioner, I believe one of the reasons lies in the fundamental approach to change communication taken by both individuals and organisations. My own work in this area has expanded my self-awareness. This helped me deal more effectively with change, loss, and grief, for myself and for the people with whom I am privileged to work. I have learned it is important to give people some time and space to deal with the impact of change, rather than expect to rush them to a positive solution.

So how can change agents help themselves and the leaders they support?

The change agent must work closely with leaders to help them overcome their own fears and concerns, so that they can embrace the change and instil confidence about the change in those around them.

Inform, Inspire, Involve

To mobilise heads, hearts, and hands, it is essential to *inform* people by providing facts, to *inspire* by tuning into people's emotions, and to *involve* people by engaging them in making things happen and to give meaning to the desired change. Look at this example from Malcolm Bollos of the Bowman Group, where a change was achieved not by talking only about targets but by making the required change visible and comprehensible to all those involved.

> When working with a crisp factory in North East England we noticed production line waste figures were represented using graphs showing % good product produced by shift by line proudly pinned up on the notice board at the end of each production line. The performance hovered between 98.0 and 98.5% good production for the past few months. I asked a line operator what these figures actually meant. She said she did not really know as she never really got to grips with percentages at school but it was clear to her that 98.5% good production was better than 98%. We watched the line manager dutifully post the figures for yesterday at the start of each shift and watched the operators never give them a second glance. This was a classic habitual ritual that you can see acted out up and down the country in any production area or indeed most offices each week.

> We tackled this by getting the performance measures to actually mean something to the target audience they were aimed at – the crisp line operators. We first discovered what they cared about and found that they were all passionate members of the 'Toon Army' – (this means they support Newcastle United football club). We calculated how many bags of crisps 1.5 – 2% production waste actually amounted to (a very large number indeed) and then got a seating plan for Sunderland's football stadium (Newcastle's fiercest rivals). We changed the measure to represent how many Sunderland supporters we could supply with free bags of crisps each week if we continued at current performance levels. We

represented this by shading in the number of seats awarded a free bag of crisps in the Sunderland stadium graphic.

This sparked the operators' imagination and in no time at all production lines were operating at 99.5% good production on the basis that 'the crisps we make are simply too good for the poor Mackems' (the derogative name Geordies give to their North East neighbours). Now in consultancy and scientific parlance this is known as the Hawthorne effect - we however simply called it the 'free crisps to the enemy effect'![4]

What Bollos and his team managed to do, simply and effectively, was to help management communicate the required change in a visible way that had meaning for the employees. In the words of Marchand and Peppard,

Business change initiatives are about engaging the minds, hearts and values of people in making change happen and achieving shared business results and benefits, not about possessing new tools, renewing legacy systems or standardising technology to reduce costs.[5]

From Cascades to Waves

While few would doubt that communication is absolutely vital in times of change, a classic mistake is to implement it in a mechanical fashion as a cascade from the top to the bottom of the organisation. According to Drucker,

For centuries we have attempted communication 'downward'. This, however, cannot work, no matter how hard and how intelligently we try. It cannot work, first because it focuses on what we want to say. Communication is the act of the recipient. What we have been trying to do is to work on the emitter, specifically on the manager, the administrator, the commander, to make him capable of being a better communicator. But all one can communicate downward are commands, that is, prearranged signals. One cannot communicate downward anything connected with understanding, let alone motivation. This requires communication upward, from those who perceive to those who want to reach their perception.[6]

Instead, it is more powerful to view communication as a series of waves that flow back and forth, creating a two-way dialogue.

Effective change agents employ three kinds of waves during change: Information, Inspiration, and Involvement.

These waves are relevant across all stages of change. When people first hear the news of a change, they are likely in a state of shock, denial, or anger. They are not listening to what is being said. Productivity and self-esteem drop as people may develop resistance, feelings of fear, panic, or sadness. They start searching for answers, rationalising the change, and questioning how they can be part of it. Finally, they are able to accept the change, seek a solution, and become fully engaged again. The three waves support people moving through the stages of the change curve.

Information is essential in helping people understand the *what* of the change - available in many formats so people can come back to it, as and when they are ready. No single communication channel can suffice. Make the information easily accessible by providing both verbal and written communication opportunities so when people search to question or rationalise the change, they can find reassurance in the consistency and availability of the message. As they find solutions to a way forward and accept the change, reattaching to the goals of the organisation, the ability to cope returns and productivity increases.

Inspiration helps to explain the *why* of the change and relates to galvanising people behind a common goal and giving them a sense of hope for the future, for themselves and the company. A common error in communicating change is being overly critical of what happened previously. Most employees were part of what happened before, so hearing criticism from senior management may elicit a defence response and make people more resistant to any proposed change. Resistance, in psychological terms, describes a motivational state consisting of distress, anxiety and desire to restore freedoms taken away when an individual responds to a perceived threat or to loss of a freedom.

According to theory when an individual feels forced into certain behaviour, they react against the coercion.[7] In my work with organisations and CEOs, I always counsel them to express 'Pride in the Past, a Passion for the Present and a Focus on the Future.' By applying this frame to communication, leaders ensure that defensive responses are reduced and can focus the brain away from the pain of the change and towards the potential benefit.

Involvement is fundamental at every stage to explain the *how* of a change and to help people work through their feelings. As a social species, humans easily feel threatened and isolated by potential or perceived consequences. According to findings by neuroscientist Naomi Eisenberger, social pain experienced through exclusion engages the same part of the brain as physical pain.[8] So when someone says they 'feel hurt,' they actually do. Involving people in decisions that affect them, no matter how small, may alleviate those feelings and lead to a reappraisal, giving an increased sense of autonomy and engagement.[9]

Adopting a communication strategy that includes information, inspiration, and involvement can dramatically improve the chance of change acceptance. Yes, it takes more time upfront to communicate the change using the waves approach; however, any time invested at this stage can reduce the length of the loss of productivity and speed up the adoption of the change.

Recognising the Pain and Selling the Gain

One myth of leadership is that people are always averse to change. Actually, people can welcome change; what they seek to avoid is the pain of change and the fear of the unknown.[10] According to David Rock, if people feel under attack, the threat evokes an avoid response in which they are likely to minimise danger, disengage, and become problem focused.[11] This leads to reduced creativity at a time when an organisation needs innovation more than ever in order to deal with difficulty. In fact, all too often employees are just focused on doing the minimum to survive. Suppressing emotion can create an even more negative environment. When people feel listened to and cared for, they are more likely to maximise reward, remain engaged, and become solution focused, thus opening up opportunities and potential.

So the challenge is to create an environment where people feel familiar with the change, can see its benefits, and feel sufficiently protected to step out of their comfort zones and dare to take risks. To create this environment, those communicating the change need to demonstrate active listening skills, as well as be able to deliver powerful messages. They have to be able to recognise the pain caused and then 'sell' the gain change will bring.[12]

People have a basic need to be heard, especially in times of stress. Creating opportunities where people can vent and put words to their emotions can actually reduce the level of emotion they are feeling.[13] I worked with a team going through a period of uncertainty during an organisational change where the company had announced that there would be changes but had not shared what they were or when they would be communicated. As a result, rumours were rife and people were very anxious about the future. We held an off-site retreat during which the leader spoke openly about his feelings and concerns. This show of vulnerability and openness was appreciated by the team, who were then able to express how they were feeling, uncovering negative, neutral, and positive emotions. We laid out a change curve on the floor and everyone stood where they felt they were and then spoke about how it felt to be in that place. Later in the session, people were then better able to let go of their concerns and focus more on what they could influence or control in the period of change. People left the retreat feeling less burdened and more positive about the future.

Active listening can be a change leader's most powerful tool. In fact, combining a supportive silence with a few key words can exhibit the empathy and caring people both need and expect. During the 2012 U.S. presidential election season, both Barack Obama and Mitt Romney halted their campaigns to focus on the impact of Superstorm Sandy and to visit affected people. They knew that, in times of crisis, expressions of perceived self-interest would not be popular. Instead, they demonstrated how much they care for people by focusing on relief efforts. Said President Obama,

> *We certainly feel profoundly for all the families whose lives have been upended. The most important message I have for them is that America's with you. We are standing behind you. And we are going to do everything we can to help you get back on your feet.*

They had learned lessons from the criticism of George Bush during Hurricane Katrina in 2005.[14]

Turning Spiders into Wolves

When I was vice president of communications at Tetra Pak, a world leader in food processing and packaging solutions, then-CEO Nick Shreiber spent a great deal of time developing leadership among the senior management. In the past, each country manager had been 'king' of his area. The top 120 were more a collection of individuals - albeit strong and successful ones - than a team. Shreiber decided to address the topic of leadership at the top management conference, which everyone attended.

We worked to find a symbol to represent that sense of both individual and team. I researched various concepts and finally we decided upon using wolves as a symbol for leadership at Tetra Pak. The wolf quote by Rudyard Kipling perfectly suited the message Nick wanted to send: 'For the strength of the pack is the wolf / And the strength of the wolf is the pack.'[15] The symbol was visual, visible, and memorable. In fact, so successful was the theme that it was extended to represent leadership throughout the company and was used for a five-year period.

One of the biggest mistakes made by those leading change is that they do not communicate enough. Without regular communication, a negative climate erodes trust and affects productivity and morale. The Tetra Pak Wolf turned into the animal model of communication. This shows leaders' reactions to change and communication (see Figure 1).

Figure 1: Animal Model

Koalas don't do much, don't say much, and are pretty ineffective (we all know some of those).

Parrot leaders speak a lot, and, at first, they can be incredibly inspiring. However, in time, people realise that there is no action to match the words and the leader loses credibility.

Most business leaders tend to fall into the spider category. They are extremely busy doing things, very action-oriented and results-focused. However, they rarely communicate. Spider leaders communicate once and think that people have understood the message or that people can find the information they need on the company's intranet. These leaders are reluctant to communicate unless they have something new to say. In the absence of new information, they become invisible, retreating to their offices and focusing on daily business.

Building on the leadership symbol, wolves are extremely social pack animals. The hierarchy in a wolf pack can equate to that of an organisation. The leader's words and actions are given disproportionate value.

Times like these, full of uncertainty, and with no new developments, bring the role of the leader in change to the fore. Change agents must encourage and train leaders to emulate the wolf, matching their walk and their talk, being aware of their body language, tone, words, and how they impact those around them. At Tetra Pak, I was part of a team who implemented a worldwide leadership communications training programme to help equip leaders and their management teams to be more effective communicators.

When Nick Shreiber was appointed as CEO of Tetra Pak in December 2000, his words and his actions were scrutinised, analysed, and given much greater symbolic meaning than his same actions and words in his prior position as President of the Americas. It became clear that the title of CEO carries significance beyond the individual. Shreiber said, "After experiencing that my words and actions impacted the organisation in more powerful ways than I had intended, I realised the symbolic power of my role, and I was then able to leverage it in service of the change process."

In contrast, when the Deepwater Horizon Oil Rig exploded in 2010, killing 11 workers and spewing oil into the Gulf of Mexico in what was the worst environmental disaster in American history, BP CEO Tony Hayward said, "We're sorry for the massive disruption it's caused to their lives. There's no one who wants this thing over more than I do, I'd like my life back." He was heavily criticised for his statements and didn't survive in the role of CEO. [16]

Change agents must work with leaders to build empathy for those affected by change, putting leaders into the shoes of others, rather than expecting others to put leaders into their shoes. Rehearsal role-plays, where change agents help leaders experience what it is like to be on the other side of a change, are a practical exercise. Filming and then viewing these role-plays can help leaders to recognise the impact of their words and actions, and to adjust their delivery and messages accordingly. Time invested in perfecting the change communication, in advance, can pay dividends in terms of benefit to the organisation.

Often, as leaders rise through the ranks, it is harder to find out the 'truth.' Leaders may be told what they want to hear, rather than be told what is actually happening or how people are really feeling. In medieval times, the king would have a court jester, someone who was no threat to the throne, who would tell him what people were saying and how things were viewed. The change agent can help leaders with change communication by filling a role similar to that of the court jester.

In 1994, British Airways actually appointed Paul Birch to the position of 'court jester.' Describing the importance of involving people and listening to feedback, Birch said,

> When things go wrong, employees usually have a good idea of how to fix them. You need to create a state in which they've got the commitment and the courage to do something. You want to build organisations where everyone sees provocation as one of their essential roles. [17]

Three Practical Steps for Effective Change Communication

Here are three practical action steps that can significantly improve the success of any change initiative, and the credibility of the change leader. While apparently common sense, rigour, discipline and action applied to these steps is what makes the difference. People talk about planning, preparing and communicating – the power is in the details, and practising.

Plan, Prepare, and Practise

When working on a change initiative, ensure that communication is involved from the start at both a strategic and operational level.

Plan

Build a clear communications plan, be sure to assess the impact of the implementation and adjust messaging, vehicles, and timings as necessary. Keep a pulse of the organisation. Talk to colleagues who are also communicating similar messages and share learning: what has worked well and what has not worked so well. Reassess during and after major communications activities and be prepared to adapt as and if required. Plan out a calendar of activity matched to your audience to ensure frequent, consistent coverage and ample opportunities for dialogue, questions, and clarification.

Prepare

Structure the frequency of change communications rather than leaving it to chance. Mix and match communications channels to maximise the available opportunities for a message to be received and understood. Use a mix of one-to-one dialogues, small group meetings, and large group meetings. Use notice boards by coffee machines, intranet, memos, e-mails, and social media where appropriate. Create Q&A documents that cover more detail and answer questions that employees are likely to ask. Openly ask for feedback and listen to the response. Make hand-outs available.

Take time to prepare your key messages. Use the acronym PACK to structure these messages.

- *Purpose* – What do you want to achieve, and why?

- *Audience* - Who are they, and what do you want from them?

- *Channels* - Which will you lead with, and which support your message?

- *Key Messages* -What are your three key points (supported with facts or examples to make them credible and engaging)?

Link messages to your overall business objectives and to the bigger organisational picture. Your communication structure should focus on the 'Head, Heart, and Hands' – what do you want people to think, feel, and do? Have in mind what you want people to say about your presentation or speech if they were interviewed as they left. When you know your core message, start with it and finish with it so that the audience is clear about what you want them to know. People remember what they hear first, what they hear last, what they hear frequently, and what touches them. In the words of Napoleon Bonaparte,

> *If I always appear prepared, it is because before entering an undertaking, I have meditated long and have foreseen what might occur. It is not genius that reveals to me suddenly and secretly what I should do in circumstances unexpected by others; it is thought and preparation.* [18]

Practise

Spend an equal amount of time practising the delivery and working on the content. In a crisis, people look to the leader to guide them through the storm. A calm, caring demeanour can speak volumes. Think about the physical layout of the venue, as well as where and how to stand, the tone of your voice, and your projection.

Visualisation is a powerful technique to help you achieve your goals in terms of a future desired outcome; used by sportspeople and actors, it is still relatively rare in the world of business. What do we mean by visualisation? Visualisation is the process of creating a mental picture of what you want to achieve. It works best when it uses as many of the senses as possible. What you imagine can include visual images and pictures, auditory aspects (sounds and words you would hear), thoughts and feelings, and even smells that may be present. The more you repeat the visualisation, the more you can train your mind and body to perform in the way you have imagined.

Create what author and public-speaking expert Peter Meyers calls "a performance preparation pattern."[19] This involves thinking about the way you stand, move and breathe, recalling a moment when you felt particularly powerful and anchoring the feeling, so that you can bring yourself into the best physical and mental state to enhance your performance.

Understand the Pain, Refocus on the Gain

Remember that in any change, the person communicating has already had time to become familiar with and adjust to the change. The people hearing about it are often hearing it for the first time, or it comes at the end of a number of rumours, shared at the coffee machine or in quiet corners.

Share decisions that affect employees quickly and respectfully. People can deal with bad news. What they find more difficult is uncertainty – 'not knowing' causes major stress. It is vital that leaders recognise that they have been aware of the change for significantly longer than their employees. Perhaps employees have even been involved in designing the change. Therefore, leaders are far further along in the process of accepting the change than the receivers of the message.

Time after time, leaders communicate changes to employees and then are disappointed when the immediate reaction is not positive. The problem is the expectation that the initial reaction will be positive. Accept that the first response may be shock and denial.

Communicate reasons for the actions and then give people time and space to adjust to the news. Recognise and address people's feelings about any change. Create opportunities to repeat the details, future focus, and 'bigger picture' message - they may not hear it the first time. It is important that leaders maintain optimism during a change. Communicate the positive effects and convey hope for the future. However, it is important not to be blindly optimistic.

A leader must balance optimism and realism to maintain the trust and confidence of employees. Deliver both good and bad news, draw attention to challenges and opportunities, and avoid sugar coating the facts. Be confident, clear, and comfortable in delivering tough messages in a caring way. If there is a perception of fairness, people are more likely to support a change even if they don't agree with it.

When a large, privately owned, multinational company needed to make tough decisions involving layoffs, it chose to communicate the mantra 'Cool Head, Warm Heart.' While the business decisions affecting people were made logically according to the business needs, the implementation was respectful. People understood that while they didn't like what was happening, the company treated people as fairly and well as possible under the circumstances.

In practical terms, our focus becomes our reality. Our brains can focus on pain, the negative, and the loss, or they can focus on the gain, the benefit, and the opportunity. Refocus people's minds on a new challenge or opportunity. It is important to 'sell the benefits of the pain,' and to rally people behind a common goal or cause that stimulates productive work. In times of layoffs, be aware of survivor syndrome - the guilt and shock of those who remain after a colleague has been let go. Re-engage and refocus employees back to a positive aspect of the business by sharing the 'What's in it for me?' in terms of why and how the change may provide personal benefits.

Use the mantra: 'Pride in the Past, Passion for the Present, Focus on the Future.' Overly criticising the past will only upset or irritate those people who were part of it. The past is what it was, and is the reason that the situation is as it is today. It cannot be changed. However, it can be respected. The present is now. It is where people can act and be engaged. Creating opportunities for people to be involved can create excitement for the present and help refocus people on the future.

Communicate Consistently, Clearly, and Visibly

Deliver a message of confidence and hope. Put any changes into perspective and frame them within the bigger picture. Use clear and simple language, with strong visual imagery to stimulate an emotional connection. The brain thinks in pictures rather than words, so presenting messages in ways people can connect with will help them stick, as in the crisp factory and the wolves examples shared earlier.

Symbols can be an important part of any change. They create a visual representation behind which people can unite. Symbols can cross languages, cultures, and functional boundaries. One multinational corporation for which I worked with used cartoon characters to communicate the new company strategy; their efforts were successful, as cartoons not only translate across all cultures but stand out in a factory or office environment.

Repetition is important – it gives time for a message to sink in and makes it more credible. As a rule of thumb, if you as leaders have not repeated the messages so often that you can recite it in your sleep, you've not repeated it enough.

The power of three is another practical rule of thumb. People can remember three things, so structure your communication around three key messages. Recognise the power of familiarity, which according to psychologist Virginia Satir is one of the most powerful motivators, even more so than comfort. Familiarity, or the lack of it, rather than simple inertia is the reason that change is often so difficult.[20]

Use the power of the narrative wherever possible - people remember stories. Warren Bennis, leading academic in the field of leadership, argues "Effective leaders put words to the formless longings and deeply felt needs of others. They create communities out of words. They tell stories that capture minds and win hearts."[21]

It is important to pay attention to your words, tone, and body language. Research shows that if body language and words expressed are inconsistent, words used account for 7% of the understood communication, tone for 38%, and body language 55%.[22] If you do not believe what you are saying, it is unlikely that your employees will. Match the words, tone, and body language so that your communication is credible.

Think carefully about the use of words and sentence construction; for example, use the positive form of a phrase rather than the negative ("Think carefully before booking travel" rather than "don't book unnecessary travel"). If you use the negative, you draw attention to it. (For example, if you tell a person not to think about a pink elephant, the brain immediately conjures up the image of a pink elephant.)

Get out of your office and be seen. One CEO of a large, global multinational company made a point of going to other people's offices rather than having everyone come to his. This visible, conscious act of making the effort to go to others was noticed by the staff and made the CEO appear more accessible. Make a point of talking to people at all levels of the organisation and creating opportunities for dialogue. When visiting other offices, take time to 'meet and greet' people and create opportunities for them to speak with you.

Make a conscious effort to provide support when needed. Encourage questions and expressions of concern. Provide ways in which employees can communicate anonymously as well as openly. When employees are sharing worries or venting, it is a sign that they care, and may be looking for guidance and solutions.

Ensure that the management team is seen as a team – united behind a common goal and supporting each other. People model the behaviour they see from above. If you remain in your office with the door locked, people may feel you have something to hide and are not willing to communicate openly with them. Consciously choose to be a wolf over a spider.

Effective change requires engaging communications

Statistics, performance indicators, and financial targets have their place in business, but to fully mobilise people, leaders need to get them working with their heads, hearts, and hands. It is essential for change agents to use communications as a strategic tool to inform, inspire, and involve employees in the success.

"Bringing Medtronic customers in to meet our team was the most important day of the year," said former Medtronic CEO Bill George.

> We have patients come in and tell their story because they resonate much more than any kind of statistics we can give. When people shared how Medtronic products have changed their lives, it gives employees that sense of meaning behind what they do. Take the heart valve worker at Medtronic who says, I'm not putting just valves together. She once told me, 'You know what makes me proudest? When I go home at night, I'm thinking about there are five thousand people alive and well and walking around leading fuller lives because of the heart valve I made.' Now she has a mission for her own life. We've aligned. She's aligned her work with her own values, she goes home and she says I worked hard. I have a life that means something.[23]

Significant energy is invested in creating the hard indicators of change. However, time spent improving your own, your leaders' and the organisation's change communications knowledge and skills is time equally well invested. Leave behind the mechanical aspects of communication and instead approach it as a strategic tool and engage with the hard and courageous work of change communications.

Work on the change messaging and narrative, involve everyone in the change process, and train leaders to be available and open for dialogue with people across all levels of the organisation. By preparing, planning, and practicing these component parts of effective change communications, you can support leaders to increase the chances of leading their organisations effectively through difficult times, keeping employees engaged, maintaining morale and productivity.

Using effective communication to inform, inspire, and involve people within the company enables people to find meaning in what they do. They mobilise themselves to think (heads), feel (hearts), and act (hands) in the best interests of themselves, the people, and the organisation.

Performance that Lasts

How leading organisations measure performance in 2050

Martin Thomas

Dear Reader, if you're unconvinced
by all the evidence evinced
that humankind consumes still more
resources than allow the poor
and earth itself to stay alive,
please save your time. But don't connive.

This chapter offers not the space
to put the world's prophetic case.
Instead we crave a little time
for those with a more open mind
to see how we can work as one
to thrive for mother earth and son.

Those of us who accept that expanding population and economic growth are breaching the limits of the natural environment and are likely to continue to do so must ask the question: "What should we do about it?"

Government and company reports alike tell us just how well they are all doing, mainly because they depend upon attracting our votes or our money to continue with their current ways. However, the evidence of expert international opinion shows that few people believe that either government or businesses are showing leadership in changing towards sustainable futures.[1]

New Visibility

Yet by the time our grandchildren are writing books like this one, say, in 2050, some issues will be considerably clearer. They will be the second generation to grow up with global social media at their fingertips, from before their schooling begins. Ubiquitous mobile computing will have captured every move and every choice. Aggregated data from these sources will feed into rich patterns of verifiable behaviour, and this will be widely available. Our grandchildren will live in a global community, and they will know it. Their social contacts will not be constrained by the distance they can walk, but by the languages they can talk. They will know the conditions of people around the world, and they will understand the power of mass peer pressure.

Transparency of information will be the accepted way of the world. Consequently, dishonesty will always be uncovered sooner or later.

Honesty and integrity will have emerged not as esoteric abstractions, but as the most effective life principles.

By the time our grandchildren are ten years old, they - and their parents - will have seen the impacts of multiple natural catastrophes as rising sea levels and unprecedented weather conditions wipe out cities and islands of perhaps millions of people.

A Question For Our Generation

Knowing that these conditions were not their fault, nor can the problems be solved in their lifetime, they will feel that their generation has been cheated by ours. Trying to exercise decentralised responsibility themselves, they will ask us; did we have no idea what was going to happen? And if so, why did we fail to prevent it?

We might say that, in retrospect, we had no global political mechanisms to take effective action, or that we never imagined it would be so disastrous, or that we expected economic growth to bail us all out. There will be many more reasons to justify our inaction.

A Surprise? Really?

Back in the reality of 2013, we already know that this scenario is a possibility. We also know that the complexity of our world means that we cannot solve the natural challenges we face with only environmental action. Social and economic issues are inextricably intertwined with environmental action. It is unacceptable to thwart the economic development of the world's poor to compensate for the overconsumption of the rich. The geographical borders we argue about today will disappear into infinitesimal, tribal insignificance in the context of the need to deal with environmental issues on a global scale.

Political resolve to deal with global issues in 2050 will still be the scarcest commodity of all. All elected officials will face challenges stretching far beyond their tenure and their individual capabilities. Collective action will be needed, requiring trust across social, economic and cultural divides in a world of declining nation states.[2]

We can be sure, however, that the explosion of available data will overwhelm the unwary and the unprepared (as Mick Yates points out in his chapter Big Data and Leadership). The world of 2013 is about to set out on a learning journey towards uncertain futures in the almost certain knowledge that the instruments it uses to measure progress and point the way will be transformed as it goes.

Looking Back from 2050

Looking back from 2050, we realise economic progress was the "true north" that guided the world until well into the twenty-first century. Economic growth was governments' primary objective, and when growth failed to materialise, governments were lost. Their social and environmental intentions depended upon economic growth.[3] The private sector generated most economic growth; its lodestone was shareholder value. Profit and cash flow pointed in that direction. Everything a business did (including much early social and environmental reporting) was validated by its impact upon shareholder value.

In 2050, all organisations will recognise that they owe a duty of care to the natural environment and to the societies (local and global) that support them.

By 2050, it will be seen that many paid lip service to this broader responsibility for 50 years, but few organisations took it enough to heart to allow a new paradigm to emerge. Leading change was thought of as the boss's task. But the turbulence of the early twenty-first century changed the rules of the game. Only a few organisations were wise enough to see that new governance structures and business models had to be driven from within, and not only from the top.

The 2050 perspective demonstrates *Beyond Crisis* as a seminal text pushing the required mindset change.[4] *Beyond Crisis* describes how the Purposeful Self-Renewing Organisation (PS-RO) of the future would capture the creativity of people in "every seat in the organisation." Innovative work methods would need to develop from within. Change leadership would demand fostering creativity, in turn, requiring new organisational values, the power fields of cohesive behaviour.

Beyond Crisis also predicted that information flows both from within and outside the organisation would need to be developed, to share current knowledge more freely and quickly throughout the organisation and beyond its boundaries. Emery and Trist spelled out these requirements in 1965 to deal with "turbulent fields."[5]

In brief, the confluence of turbulent external conditions and the shortage of internal capacity to deal with changes imposed upon reflective leaders a new way of working. Social, environmental, and financial pressures cried out for change. Information technology created knowledge databases every month exceeding all known facts before the end of the twentieth century.

Back to the Present

In the 1980s, I led corporate planning activities in a Top Ten multinational business. I experienced directly how the planning system and its performance measurement concepts shaped strategic change and how (at the same time) they perpetuated the status quo. As CEO of a division of a different multinational in the early 2000s, I saw my earlier findings corroborated.

Old paradigms were encrusted in the processes and performance metrics of the future plans. Scenarios of radically different futures or new contextual pressures were denied. Consequently, corporate plans were not just irrelevances, or "rain dance rituals;" they functioned like blinkers, preventing the organisation from seeing any future outside their conventional tunnel of vision.

If "return on equity" is the overriding objective, people will strive for just that, particularly if their bonuses depend upon it. If you turn a blind eye to the costs of accomplishing that goal, you should not be surprised if those costs escalate. Setting performance measurement objectives in a complex context is no simple task. But it remains an enduring truth that "what gets measured gets done." We therefore need to learn to measure that which needs to get done. This is the opposite of projecting forward the performance measurements of past success.

Broader Perspectives

Those same constraints today play out on a much broader stage. Performance measurement is the domain of the investment analyst community. Even young trainee business leaders ask how their view of the world's future can be "sold" to the hard-nosed analysts who seek only short-term financial gain, often from very short-term holdings.

When the leader of the World Business Council for Sustainable Development argues for a capitalist revolution to include social, environmental and economic capital (as Peter Bakker did in 2012), the time has come to think about what has to change before the world changes us all.

Change Leaders ask what has to change and how do they accomplish that change? Five changes we can expect in the coming decades and suggestions to organisation leaders on how to become effective change leaders, follow.

1. Embrace Triple Bottom Line (3BL)[6]

That only money matters is a great fallacy underlying the 2013 status quo. Good performance should deliver a return on invested capital, but it is not by making the sole goal profit that great organisations thrive.

Enlightened businesses recognise this and say so. They thrive because they excel at meeting certain societal needs, creating more value for customers and consumers than the resources used, including social and environmental assets.

At present, the cost of social and environmental resources is not charged to their financial accounts, nor do most accounting practices provide for their replacement. Universities, hospitals, government institutions, and non-governmental organisations recognise their own financial constraints but aim to create social value in excess of their used resources.

There is a widespread recognition of the need to apply the capital maintenance principles (used in respect to financial capital for 500 years) to environmental capital and social capital, too. The idea of maintaining these three capitals, economic, social, and environmental, has been termed Triple Bottom Line (3BL).[6] These capitals do not need to be monetised to be counted.

In 2013, it is not easy for most people to conceptualise 3BL, let alone to implement it. By 2050 organisation and business leaders will need to articulate the balance between these competing objectives and constraints explicitly.

The 3BL concept will challenge many existing values. For example, we need to develop more respect for the global good, sometimes at the cost of individual benefits, particularly in parts of the world consuming more than our proportionate share of global resources. Developing new values is no simple or comfortable task, but making values explicit is a means of developing coherent values that are relevant and widely shared. The process may take several generations, so the sooner we start, the better.

We can be change leaders in our own families. Future generations can learn new values from their parents and grandparents, though we may be struggling ourselves to practise the values we know the world needs.

While money may be a convenient measure for some elements of 3BL performance, there are more meaningful metrics to use in some social and environmental performance measurements, like employee competencies and CO_2 emissions.

2. Ask "How Much Is Enough?"

Organisations go to great lengths to report their social work and their eco-efficiencies. Many of these actions are laudable; however, leaders and the public need to ask, "How much is required for this activity to be sustainable?" The answer is often not known. Leading organisations choose to do the hard work thinking about how to measure sustainable performance. They set norms of performance that meet the thresholds of sustainability.[7]

Organisations and accounting professions will find ways to answer this question. No doubt they will draw on the wave of information flowing from the Big Data tsunami. The precision of the answers will improve over time. Asking the question and documenting the answers give organisations (and their auditors) many insights. Based upon these norms and actual performances, they will soon determine what actions are required to meet the thresholds of sustainability.

If they don't ask these questions, leaders, stakeholders, and the concerned public allow reporting institutions to seek data that fails to answer the vital question. Consider this: Is it better to be approximately right than precisely wrong?

Recent surveys consistently indicate that governments are the least active institutions in leading towards sustainable futures.[1] Businesses are at the bottom of the list, too. Waiting for political leadership is not likely to answer the question, what is enough? Business leaders need to ask themselves and their stakeholders what sufficiency looks like.

3. Engage With Stakeholders[8]

Enlightened organisations have engaged in some form of communication with some of their stakeholders for many years. But often this was in a way that Chris Argyris calls this Model 1 behaviour: "Be in unilateral control. Win; do not lose. Suppress negative feelings. Act as rationally as possible."[9] Now is the time we need to move towards Model 2, to create internal commitment throughout the organisation and beyond, requiring "mistaken assumptions to be reformulated, incongruities reconciled, incompatibilities resolved, vagueness specified, untestable notions made testable, scattered information brought together into meaningful patterns and previously withheld information shared."

To do this, organisations need to engage actively with other organisations, often from other social spheres. Listening to stakeholders is indispensable. An organisation needs to consider opportunities for the co-creation of value that stakeholders seek. Listening also allows the organisation "to see ourselves as other see us", but ignore this imperative at your peril.

If a CEO commits to "protecting the communities wherever we operate", it is an empty promise unless the organisation has practical mechanisms to listen to its stakeholders and to translate this local input into real action. This is no trivial task. It takes years, and requires a tolerance for learning by trial and error.

To set the organisation's thresholds for sustainable performance, top management must consider the duties that stakeholders perceive they are owed. The organisation will need to judge itself regarding its own norms. Often various stakeholders' desires are mutually exclusive or at least incompatible. Top management must decide which action(s) to undertake. Decisions made with full stakeholder engagement will be accepted as higher quality than those made in ignorance of facts and perceived duties. Stakeholders need to be informed of decisions and outcomes. Leaders now need to ask for this framework in which to make their strategic decisions. By 2050 it should be the norm.

4. Appreciate Moral and Ethical Duties Owed

Traditional performance evaluation techniques focusing on profit are based on legal duties. In 2013, there are no contracting parties to represent the environment and few who represent vital social capitals. Organisations appreciating the need for environmental and social responsibility look for non-legal (rather, moral or ethical) duties. The initial impetus comes from the organisations' leaders, and key stakeholders help identify such duties in a local context. Without this recognition of their duty to accept non-legal responsibilities, organisations remain in the "business as usual" model of financial primacy, whatever the cost to others.

In 2012, companies in the UK and the US were shocked to be asked to take moral duties into account. Taxation authorities did not accuse them of unethical behaviour in extreme tax avoidance, but rather, customer-stakeholders were disappointed to discover just how little tax some corporations paid. Aggressively seeking to pay the legal minimum taxes, companies undermined their reputational assets. Customer-stakeholders reshaped their perception of company brand, a key intangible asset at the heart of many organisations. Leaders wishing to cultivate the reputation of good citizenship required by their stakeholders develop moral compasses, evaluating duties that extend beyond legal requirements.

While some argued that it was unethical or even illegal to spend money on anything that did not directly enhance shareholders' financial value, the 2006 Companies Act in the UK (and similarly the introduction of "B Corporations" in the US) made it explicit that directors must take account of the impact of their organisation on the environment and communities.[10]

In 2050, recognition of moral and ethical duties will be commonplace. It will be glaringly obvious that the social infrastructure relies upon products and services of businesses all around the world. The notion that businesses' primary duty is to financial investors (while social and environmental capitals decay) will appear ludicrous. Many social and environmental duties will in due course become legal requirements. Organisations satisfied with mere compliance will be followers; leaders will be those with a well-developed and road-tested moral compass. Organisations will learn to articulate their values and ensure they are implemented.

5. Think Global & Integrated

"Financial information is not sufficient. We have to provide information on sustainability, on social issues and environment, and it has to be done in an integrated way with a financial report."

Goran Tidstrom, President of the International Federation of Accountants and member of the International Integrated Reporting Council (IIRC)

Established in 2010, the International Integrated Reporting Council (IIRC) provides global coordination for economic, environmental and social performance measures. The IIRC initially focuses upon large corporations listed on stock exchanges around the world whose primary goal is to meet the needs of their financial investors.[11] However, the concept of integrated reporting applies to all organisations, not just those in the private sector.

By 2050 global impacts on all three "capitals" will be reported in a single integrated "document."[12] (This "document" may consist of online access to integrated databases, with consistent data definitions and boundaries.) Performance standards answering the question "What represents the sustainable threshold?" will be the norm.

CEOs will explain their sustainability performance annually to all stakeholders, including:

- Principles upon which the performance standards have been set, including context
- Extent to which actual performance has met the sustainability criteria
- Future expectations of progress towards meeting all standards
- Independent assurance including the audit of narrative reports and their underlying data

In 2013, it is difficult to imagine that reliable external reporting to stakeholders can advance faster than the development of meaningful metrics and processes for internal decision making. However hungry the investment community may be, meaningful sustainability reporting to markets will lag behind the development of management information measuring sustainable performance.

Since both sustainability reporting and metrics for sustainability are embryonic in 2013, it will be important to adopt common principles to be applied in a meaningful way in each local context in which an organisation operates. The alternative is to set defined metrics or key performance indicators centrally, that allow strict data comparison globally, but leave them devoid of meaning through lack of principle or context.

By 2050 therefore we may expect 3BL context-based standards to be the language of organisations of all sorts across the whole world.

Establish and Use Context-Based Norms

McElroy and van Engelen published *Corporate Sustainability Management: The Art and Science of Managing Non-Financial Performance* in 2012.[7] This seminal book on non-financial performance measurement was one of the first to propose setting thresholds for sustainability performance by engaging with stakeholders.

The underlying principle is that performance thresholds need to be set that represent a sustainable performance in the context of each organisation. The process is called Context-Based Sustainability (CBS). The essential concept is sufficiency (what represents enough?).

The following explanation borrows from Mark McElroy's text and the website of the Center for Sustainable Organisations (where worked examples are available).

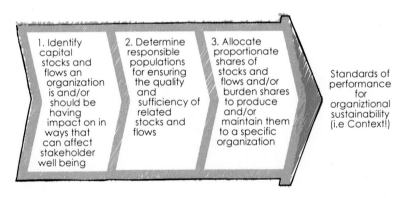

Figure 1: Logic of Determining Context

The determination of context in organisational settings is a three-step process. The first step is to determine which vital capital resources in the world an organisation is having impact upon, or should be having impact on, in ways that can affect stakeholder well-being. Identify the vital capitals.

The second step is to determine who is responsible for preserving and maintaining the vital capitals involved. Who should look after those vital capitals?

The third step is to determine what an organisation's proportionate duties and obligations are, in order to impact vital capitals, given the results of the first and second steps. What is "our" share of the capital maintenance duties?

Those duties, once endorsed by the organisation, become its Context-Based Metrics and standards for sustainable performance. These are the reference points against which actual performances are compared. Shortfalls represent unsustainable performance. Meeting or improving upon the standard is a sustainable performance. It is yes or no!

Integrated Context-Based Sustainability

Integrated Context Based Sustainability (ICBS) includes financial norms. Although McElroy and van Engelen's book deals explicitly with only non-financial performance, I worked with Mark McElroy in 2012-2013 to apply the same process to financial capital maintenance. The purpose of this work was to complete a coherent approach applicable to all three elements of the 3BL. It is a truism that no organisation can be sustainable unless it is financially sustainable. Initial indications are that the process works well with financial stakeholders, adding new insights and a new dimension to the existing economic performance measurements.

The completion of the CBS process for application to all three elements of the bottom line allows for the first time a balancing mechanism that truly integrates the reporting process. The sustainability balance mechanism is central to management information and at the heart of the 2050 organisation.

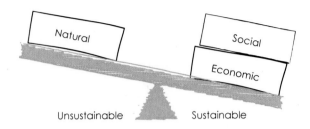

Figure 2:   The Sustainability balance mechanism

Using the norms for sustainable performance, organisations can compare actual performance and see at a glance in which areas they fall short.

This framework allows organisations to rebalance targets for future performance to enable resources from areas of over-performance to be re-allocated for addressing shortfall areas.

This vital process uses integrated reporting and decision making to address areas of need. It allows adoption of a forward-looking approach. The same balances can be drawn up to depict the anticipated future sustainability situation which results from rebalancing of resources and efforts.

While Integrated CBS offers the first practical tool to determine sustainable performance, the sustainability balance gives organisations a visual display of how to redress any shortfalls. Such navigational tools for setting strategic direction and for monitoring progress along the way are expected to be routine in 2050 organisations.

Information systems, data, and decision making like this cannot be switched on at short notice. Systems and people need to be developed over decades.

Organisations may choose to do more than survive. Thriving organisations are both sustainable and create sufficient value to prosper by creating new capital in the area of their choosing. For a university this may be knowledge capital; for a business, economic capital; for a forestry business, it may be restoring or renewing natural resources, its environmental capital. Unless the organisation exceeds its sustainability norms in its chosen area of excellence, it is only surviving and not thriving.[13]

Using this framework of Integrated Context Based Sustainability performance measurement metrics, it is feasible to set challenging targets for value creation in any one or more of the three capitals or any of their sub-divisions. For example, to maintain the reputation (a social capital) of a hospital has three component elements - patient experiences, clinical excellence, and resource effectiveness – the hospital may set sustainability standards that it can comfortably meet. However, it may choose to set higher and aspirational targets required to improve its reputation, for example in clinical excellence. This may be the decision that sparks the enthusiasm of consultant surgeons and cleaning staff alike that take it from a sustainable entity to a thriving success.

ICBS and balancing frameworks are not instruments of levelling down, they are indicators of performance that allow strategic choices to be made, resourced, implemented, and followed up. By 2050 these tools and their subtle use will be completely engrained in many organisations.

Moving Outside the Organisational Boundary

Sustainability practitioners know that the boundaries of their own organisational entity (called Scope 1) are neither the boundaries of their influence nor the boundaries of sustainability performance.

Sustainability has three scopes: the organisational entity itself (Scope 1), its inbound supply chain (Scope 2), and its outbound supply chain (Scope 3).

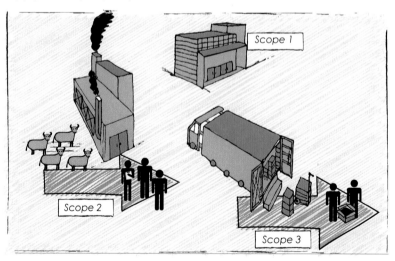

Figure 3: Three Scopes of the Supply Chain

Scope 2, the inbound supply chain, includes not only direct suppliers of materials and services, but their suppliers and the suppliers of those suppliers. A manufacturer of shoes has a Scope 2 that includes the suppliers of leather and rubber. Their suppliers include farmers of the cattle from which the leather was produced; tanneries that processed the leather; rubber plantations; and processors that treated the raw material to produce the characteristics of colour and texture required.

The outbound supply chain (Scope 3) extends to and beyond the boundaries of the customer, to include the person who uses the product or service, including disposal of packaging materials and empty, used containers.

When PUMA presented their 2011 Environmental Profit and Loss ((E)P&L) account analysis, their inbound supply chain's environmental impact represented about ten times the impact of their own Scope 1 activities.

Attempting to de-link growth from environmental impact including Scopes 1, 2, and 3, Unilever estimated that the scale of the work involved in managing the Scope 2 process was thirty times as great as Scope 1, and another thirty times as great including Scope 3.

The closed loop cycle of designing, recycling, and recapture of materials from used items ("cradle to cradle") links Scope 3 to Scope 2 and feeds back into Scope 1.[14] Hardin Tibbs argues that this cyclical approach is essential to replace the "linearity" of the supply chain concept, essentially one of "cradle to grave."[15]

Designing re-use and recycling across the extended supply chain requires a gigantic change of mindset from our present ways of working. Recapturing used materials from jettisoned consumer goods and industrial processes demands holistic thinking and active cooperation among all suppliers, distributors, customers and users. But it has huge benefits in re-using scarce materials, as well as reducing waste; consequently relieving the natural environment from much of its burden as a waste sink.

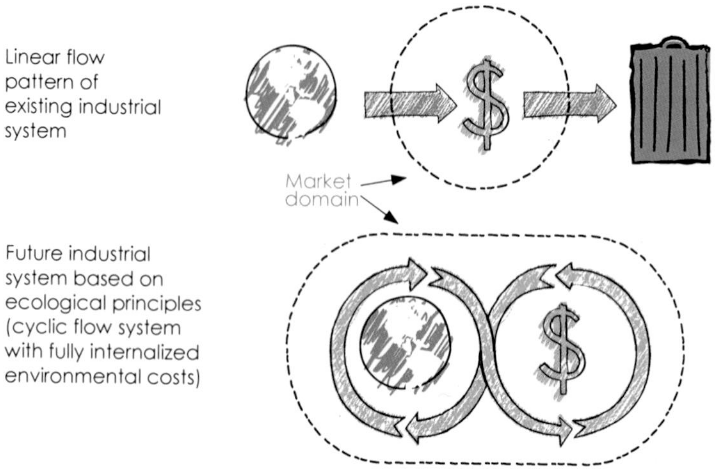

Linear flow
pattern of
existing industrial
system

Market
domain

Future industrial
system based on
ecological principles
(cyclic flow system
with fully internalized
environmental costs)

Original: Hardin Tibbs with permission

Figure 4: Moving from a linear to a closed loop world

Managing inbound and outbound supply chains requires completely different approaches. The leading entity may have influence, but it certainly does not have control of the process.[16] The exercise of influence across a network becomes a core competency and by 2050 will be perhaps the most critical ability for managing change.

In order to influence organisations over which control cannot be exercised, commonality of principles (including principles of sustainability performance measurement) is more important than commonality of detailed definitions. Principles can be applied across organisations that are controlled as well as those in the extended supply chain.

Integrated Context-Based Sustainability principles are designed to allow individual organisations to develop their own meaningful definitions of vital capitals and the relevant impacts. They allow local operators to apply common principles allowing them to work with suppliers and customers. If suppliers and customers each specify the metrics to be applied and the means of collecting the data to meet those requirements, a plethora of detailed requirements will result, and that would be a disaster.

Imagine for example that Walmart, Tesco, and Carrefour each have different definitions of required data from their suppliers. Each common supplier would have to produce data meeting all three sets of data definitions, and this requirement would have to be cascaded to every link in each suppliers' supply chains. The administrative burden upon suppliers' suppliers would be immense – and confusing.

By 2050, organisations of all sorts will report on their own Scope 1 sustainability performance - as well as Scopes 2 and 3. To avoid strangling organisations with multiple data definitions and reporting incompatibilities, we must set standards at the level of global principles and allow meaningful data and metrics to be developed in the local context.

How Does This 2050 Mini- Scenario Help Change Leaders to Lead Change in the Twenty Teens?

This is merely a scenario. Scenarios never come to fruition completely. However, they can have sufficient substance in descriptions of the world and of the 2050 organisation to enable change leaders today to gain a sense of how different it will be from here and now. This glimpse of the future should foster an understanding of the depth and breadth of organisational building work required to realise that future. Scenarios as a methodology show possible futures. Their power lies in the way in which they allow today's leaders to consider which futures may emerge. Leaders help create the future, prepare to influence it and adapt to whatever may occur. The choices they make as they lead change will result in more or less successful outcomes.

In the 1970s, Shell began to use scenarios in this way, and it credits this tool with helping the company avoid much of the pain of the 70s oil crisis. In the 90s various governments have found it useful: Singapore use scenarios successfully to design social and governance policy, while South Africa credits scenarios in the decision to step down from apartheid. Scenarios are big pictures made human size.

9 Global Trends Influencing the World of 2050

Scarce Resources

Population Growth

Ubiquitous Computing

Transparency Everywhere

Honesty & Integrity are Norms

Decentralised Responsibility

Complexity

Big Data

Turbulence

The side bar lists the key characteristics referred to throughout this chapter. It is deceptively simple. Nine global trends shape the world of 2050. These in turn lead to eleven key characteristics of the Organisation of 2050 (on next page) and represent a major sustained transformation from where most organisations are today.

Explore the Path to 2050

As a programmatic approach, scenarios offer leaders an opportunity for simple backcasting, a scenario based technique to work from a scenario way out in the future, back to present time.

For each of the 11 organisational characteristics, draw a line from the 2050 organisation back to today in your organisation. What stages must your organisation go through to be able to fulfil the condition described? Think backwards seeing each decade as a stage from 2050 to 2040, 2030, and on to today. This gives a sense of the different stages of change to be made and helps focus into 'what must be done today'. Focuses on where to start and initiate projects today to ensure a thriving sustainable organisation for 2050.

Another way of helping organisations is to use metrics based on the sustainability balance as a prioritisation framework. Choose an aspect of the organisation that you feel deserves the highest priority and start to engage with stakeholders to focus attention. There is also a benefit in taking the prime mover position. Being a pioneer in any peer group delivers benefits including setting standards and procedures that are adopted by followers.

My personal preference is to spend some time "camping" with each of those future characteristics. Allow the mind to wander from one to another and to think of the links between them. If that gives a glimpse of a future as yet unseen and unthought-of, it will have served its purpose. The pace of future change is on a different order of magnitude to that of past decades. The turbulence of today's world makes dealing with change all the more demanding. But the prize to those who can adapt fast will be there for the taking. As attributed to Darwin "It is not the strongest of the species that survives, nor the most intelligent, but the one most responsive to change."

Using the sustainability balancing mechanism, Integrated Context-Based Sustainability (ICBS) and performance management

11 Organisational Characteristics Influencing Organisation 2050

Innovative PS-RO

Explicit Shared Values

Triple Bottom Line

Context Based Norms

Stakeholder Engagement

Moral Compass Road Test

Think Global & Integrated

Balance & Rebalance 3BL

Targeted Thriving

Scopes 1, 2 & 3

Global Principles: Local Norms

processes offers a way forward that helps organisations do more than survive in 2050.

Please bear in mind that innovation and leadership must be allowed to come from any seat in the organisation. Dear Reader: nothing less will do the job!

Organisation 3.0

The future of large enterprises

*Silke Grotegut, Anja Reitz, and
Wulf Schönberg*

Introduction

The major challenges of fast-changing workplaces and markets driven by changing demographics, globalisation and technological innovation are dynamics and complexity. Yet most companies are still structured for efficiency, which is no longer the greatest problem. In large companies, creativity is needed to tackle development of services and products, and to find innovative solutions faster than competitors do.

It is crucial for companies to meet the following challenges: speed, flexibility, innovation, and a fitting company culture. We will explore and provide answers about how a company's evolving structure can meet these challenges. Large companies especially must undergo cultural shifts because they are often like big oil tankers - they change course slowly and are ineffective in a rapidly changing work environment. (For our purposes, large companies are corporate groups with complex products and services, and more than 100,000 employees, like many telecommunication and information technology firms)

"Organisation 3.0" symbolises the development of future organisational designs and models for large companies. A new perspective on the purpose and format of organisational structures acts as a reference point. Our organisational design principles focus on self -responsibility and increasing freedom for both leaders and employees. Large companies can become more flexible, react faster to market changes and innovate accordingly, and increase their attractiveness to current and future employees.

We'll look at trends driving a new style of organisation, Org 3.0, describe its key qualities and then share our own experience in a traditional metrics-focused hierarchical organisation as we seek to create Org 3.0.

Future Trends

The economy and working environments are experiencing increasing competition, speed, and complexity. Futurologists like Lynda Gratton[1] and Matthias Horx[2] assert the following megatrends for the future:

- Demographic changes
- Globalisation
- Technological development
- Knowledge-based society and specialisation
- Change in societal values

As many of us are in the midst of these trends, we highlight the pertinent ones shaping Organisations 3.0.

Demographic Change

In Europe the average citizen's age and the declining birth rate will result in shrinking populations and a waning number of people of employable age[3]. Employees will have to work until an older age (which will compensate for the pension reduction), but not only because people live longer, and are fitter till older ages, they also *want* to continue to work, to use their knowledge and experience[4]. In addition, the economy demands more highly skilled personnel – that is, the older generations.

Demographic development is also closely connected to women's changing societal role. More women achieve higher education levels and statistically, the higher the education level attained, the fewer children a woman is likely to have. A study from Mathews and Ventura "based on an analysis of 1994 birth certificates, found a direct relationship between years of education and birth rates, with the highest birth rates among women with the lowest educational attainment."[5]

Work life in general grows more dynamic, and family structures are changing: in addition to the classical, nuclear family, there are now, for example, blended families, DINKs (Double Income, No Kids), and single-parent households. Work and life instabilities pressure young employees: they feel they have to achieve a great deal from ages 20 to 40, and many of them try to reduce the pressure by foregoing family. Expectations for family-work balance, career focus, and the need for a double income all factor into this changing environment[6].

Globalisation[7]

Globalisation is the phenomenon of the expanding world economy, in which everyone can obtain everything at any time wherever they are. Time, locale, and borders do not matter anymore. Goods and services are provided globally and the labour market will open up for people worldwide. Employers will have an international talent pool, and job candidates will face competition from all over the world. In addition, emerging economies gain prominence and economic strength based on projected growth in world trade. This will affect individual economies and thus parts of multinational organisations unevenly[8].

Technological Development[9]

Knowledge continues to increase exponentially, spurring further technological development, which will in turn increase productivity. We already observe that while products and services are growing more complex, product life cycles are shorter. New forms of collaboration are necessary - crowdsourcing to try to solve intricate problems is increasingly popular. Continuing technological development will increase the need for highly skilled professionals, while the need for unskilled workers decreases. In developing countries and emerging markets low-cost innovation will be important, as their populations are eager to participate in technological development.

Knowledge Based Society and Specialisation

In the last 100 years the percentage of agricultural and blue collar workers decreased significantly, while the number of service providers and/or white collar workers (in areas such as management, consulting, and research) grew[10] Increasing technology and the general fact that global knowledge availability is doubling every 5 to 7[11] years makes specialisation necessary[12]. With this rising degree of required specialisation increases the need for communication, because complex services and products require the cooperation of specialists.

The human knowledge base grows exponentially as information is digitalised. It is available everywhere. Informal training is possible wherever a teacher or technology is available, e.g. AcademicEarth.org posts courses online for free from Top Universities like Stanford or MIT. Education is become more and more independent of social origin. An increasing knowledge base connects to innovation, the precondition for large companies' future success.

Change in Societal Values[13] [14]

Generation Y - people born between 1981 and 1991 - value work/life balance, family time, freedom for creativity, and, especially, purpose. They have a strong affinity for technical developments, are used to working in virtual teams, and do not accept hierarchy. Gen Yers require individualism and flexibility without the abdication of job security (called "flexicurity"). This generation must cooperate with the Gen Xers (people born 1960-1980) and the baby boomers (post-World War II, 1946-1964), both of whom value instead duty, performance, discipline, desire for consistency, and a strong job focus[15]. Millennial (those born 1991-2000+) are beginning to enter the work force and will add their own generational culture to the organisation.

Additionally customer values also change, and sustainable products and production methods gain importance as ecological consciousness grows.

These megatrends will change the whole work environment, and these future challenges will influence large companies in many ways.

The most important impacts on the working world include:

- War for talent: a lack of experts due to demographic change (skills shortage);
- Employee demands for more responsibility and autonomy, and the importance of self-realisation ("Gen Y");
- Growing importance of values (not limited to sustainability, cooperation, creativity, and ecological consciousness);
- Longer work-life and life spans;
- Different generations and nationalities with different mind sets working simultaneously in the value chain;
- Rise of complexity in the working world, while specialisation levels of employees increase;
- Ever-growing demand for 24/7 availability of increasingly digitised knowledge; capability to work anywhere, anytime; and
- Increasing impact of social media in the work environment.

Challenges for the Future

The industrial revolution made mass production of goods possible and, according to Niels Pfläging, markets were characterised by long product life cycles; few changes; stable prices; and loyal customers. [16]

The major challenge was to produce goods efficiently, and in order to do so, mass production companies structured their organisations in a Tayloristic line form with a strong differentiation between management and staff. Henry Ford's quote exemplifies the power suppliers held then: "Any customer can have a car painted any colour that he wants as long as it is black".

Today suppliers do not have that power - the customers do. The resulting highly competitive markets are characterised by disruptive changes; short product life cycles; permanent price pressure by the market; high financial expectations by shareholders; and very demanding but disloyal customers.

Organisational Answers for these Challenges

Overview of Current Organisational Models

Review of the literature and practical examples reveal different organisational structures today. The following four different models are typical: line organisation/matrix organisation; project organisation; entrepreneurial organisation and the hybrid.

Line organisation and matrix organisation

Line and matrix organisations are characterised by a hierarchical system; functional, regional, or customer-related structure; many routine tasks; and a focus on efficiency (This is typical for many large companies nowadays). [17]

Project organisation

Project organisations are established for only a certain period of time, and their staff come from different disciplines. These organisations usually have clearly defined goals and a set timeframe within which to achieve them (e.g. construction projects). [18]

| Entrepreneurial organisation |

According to Friedrich Glasl, entrepreneurial organisations are in the pioneer phase.[19] They are rife with improvisation and chaos, usually focused on one person (the pioneer). They are flexible and innovative, based on new ideas, and very close to the customer - even, sometimes, interlaced with the customer (e.g. Apple in its beginning phase).

| Hybrid Organisational types |

Recent literature also describes "hybrid"[20], network, "virtual" (or decentralised) organisational models; and "holocratic,"[21] "heterarchic," or "shamrock"[22] organisations.

Network and Hybrid Organisations

Network and hybrid organisations are, from our point of view, the most important modern developments in organisational structure.

Network (decentralised or virtual) organisations are typically organisations functioning online (in the virtual world), driven by common values and norms.[23] They are flexible, open, undetermined systems.[24] There is no management and no hierarchy, and responsibility fluctuates. Members can drop in and drop out as they wish. Well-known network organisations are Alcoholics Anonymous and Wikipedia. Network organisational structure, while effective in the voluntary sector, is not suitable for for-profit companies. [25] Hybrid organisations are described in a variety of ways in the literature; however, we use this term similarly to the way we use Branfman's "starfish and spider organisation."[25]

Branfman and Beckstrom differentiate between centralised and decentralised organisations. In centralised (spider) organisations, the power is concentrated with management. Employees have to wait for decisions and orders, and they are not involved in decision-making. Because management is not familiar with client needs, with production processes, or with local customs, this often entails protracted decision-making processes and final decisions that do not fit – or fix - the problem. Branfman and Beckstrom use the imagery of a spider because a spider cannot exist without a brain, and the body must follow the brain's decisions. In comparison, a starfish is a network of autonomous cells, with no brain. These cells must reach consensus on any action, and, if divided into pieces, none die - each piece goes on living individually.

When we speak about this imagery in relation to companies, decentralised organisations are a network of autonomous, self-responsible cells following one common purpose e.g. developing software, such as Linux. These organisations are flexible and adapt rapidly to the changing environment or customer needs.

Hybrid organisations combine aspects of decentralised and centralised organisations. Amazon, eBay, Google, Facebook, and Wikipedia are hybrid organisations. They each have a headquarters that frames the business and the company's purpose, and they have one chairman representing the company. However, these companies have decentralised characteristics as well.

For example, "eBay hosts user-to-user interaction and relies on a decentralised user rating system, the company itself is no starfish ... it has a CEO, a headquarters, a hierarchy and well-defined structure ... It's neither a pure starfish nor a pure spider, but what we call a hybrid organisation ... Companies like eBay combine the best of both worlds– the bottom-up approach of decentralisation an the structure, control, and resulting profit potential of centralisation. EBay is a centralised company that decentralises the customer experience. When it comes to pay, eBay uses PayPal, its own subsidiary, which is based on rigid controls and secure interactions."[26]

Hybrid organisations have in common the responsibility shift to the company's periphery, to employees close to markets and the customer, or even directly to the customer.

They decentralise "elements by giving their customers a role: eBay turned over the policing of the site to its users, Amazon encouraged any reader – however educated or well read – to review book titles"
[27]

Management is replaced with coordination; decisions are made by the most competent person for the task, hierarchy and responsibility fluctuate from case to case.

	Line Organization	Project Organization	Hybrid Organization	Entrepreneur Organization	Network Organization*
Company Characteristics	▫ Efficiency driven ▫ Recurring tasks ▫ Routine ▫ Reducing complexity ▫ Risk reducing ▫ Solving known problems ▫ Extremely hierarchical ▫ Mass production	▫ Effectivity driven ▫ Focused on business development ▫ Monitoring risks ▫ Task linking ▫ Increasing complexity ▫ Responsible for the whole ▫ Learning & Growth-oriented ▫ Projects (e.g. bldg. sector)	▫ Effective driven ▫ Integrating environment; strong permeability between inside and outside ▫ Focused on expert exchange and development ▫ Complexity increasing ▫ Social Media using ▫ Organizations like eBay, Amazon, Toyota	▫ Improvisation, flexibility ▫ Strong affected by enterepreneur ▫ New ideas and innovation ▫ Chaos ▫ Strong bondance between org and customers ▫ Deep knowledge about customers ▫ Start ups. creative cells	▫ Effectivity driven ▫ Driven by common values and norms ▫ Flexibility ▫ Complexity increasing ▫ Social Media using ▫ Open and undetermined system ▫ Virtual organization, Communities, NPO
Org. Characteristics	▫ Line or matrix org. ▫ Process oriented ▫ A lot of secondary org. ▫ Top-down Leadership ▫ Clear decision process ▫ Tayloristic division of work ▫ Distinctive hierarchy	▫ Polydimensional steering ▫ Temporary decision processes ▫ Focused on market dynamic & complexity ▫ Interdisciplinary	▫ Both, centralized and decentralized elements ▫ Coordination instead of management ▫ Fluctuating hierarchy and responsibility ▫ Focused on market dynamic and complexity ▫ Interdisciplinary & specialization	▫ Little structure ▫ No secondary organization ▫ Paternalistic leadership ▫ No process orientation and functional differentiation ▫ No job evaluation	▫ Autonomy of participation ▫ No management ▫ No hierarchies ▫ Fluctuating responsibilities ▫ Strong focus on values ▫ Interdisciplinary

Central Bureaucratic Hierarchic — Decentral Post Bureaucratic Heterarchic

LEGEND: Frequency Today / Prognosted Frequency

Based on F.Glasl, 1942; Brantman et al.
* equivalent:decentral or starfish organizations

Figure 1: Different organization models and their characteristics

Large companies today are mainly line organisations, but as mentioned before, the Tayloristic line organisation is a suitable structure for industrial mass markets. With the emergence of the knowledge-based economy, however, the Tayloristic line organisation is not suitable anymore.

Layers of Structure in an Organisation

Large companies usually have many more layers than simply a formal line structure. According to Niels Pfläging, every organisation consists of an informal structure (interconnection based on personal relationships – in other words: people networks) and a value creation structure (a network of functions interrelated by value flow). [28]

Often the value chain is buried under the formal structure and thus is not clear to managers. Since the formal structure normally groups in functions, regions, or products, but does not follow the value chain, the informal structure is often used to maintain a value chain.

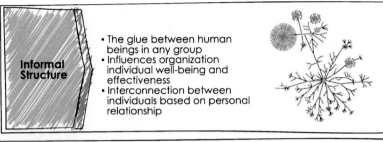

Informal Structure
- The glue between human beings in any group
- Influences organization individual well-being and effectiveness
- Interconnection between individuals based on personal relationship

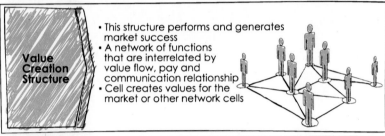

Value Creation Structure
- This structure performs and generates market success
- A network of functions that are interrelated by value flow, pay and communication relationship
- Cell creates values for the market or other network cells

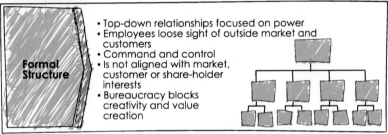

Formal Structure
- Top-down relationships focused on power
- Employees loose sight of outside market and customers
- Command and control
- Is not aligned with market, customer or share-holder interests
- Bureaucracy blocks creativity and value creation

Based on Niels Pfläging

Figure 2: Three layers of structure in an organization.

Organisational Criteria for the Future

"Organisation 3.0" (Org 3.0) aims to reduce the energy needed to build and administer a company's formal structure, instead to concentrate energy on the value chain. Org 3.0 gives value-creating units a high level of autonomy and decision-making. They must organise themselves and take full responsibility for their action as a unit, as a team, and as individuals. Gen Yers find a higher degree of freedom and the possibility for professional self-actualisation attractive, and also useful as resumé points in future employment searches.

Criteria for Successful 3.0 Organisations

Three criteria stand out for a successful network Org 3.0 business: a value-chain orientated organisation, self-responsible teams, and distribution of power to the operative units.

Value-chain orientated organisation

Value-chain orientated organisations bring together functions along the value-chain. In a function-oriented structure, tasks that belong together are grouped into different functions (e.g. Sales, HR, Controlling, and Purchasing), requiring coordination time, different targets, and so on. Most notably, it leads to the problem that the same task can fall under different areas of responsibility, because in a value-chain orientated organisation, all functions needed are implemented in one organisational unit and are focused on one value chain.

Self-responsible teams

Implementation of self-responsible teams implies reduction of management levels, and their replacement via social/team, rather than hierarchical control. Headquarters is only involved for devolving functions (e.g. auditing) or if operative units do not have the competence to make decisions. In the classical model these are normally centralised. In Org 3.0 individuals, teams and units are given much greater responsibility. Semco[29], a Brazilian conglomerate, for example delegates the responsibility for budgeting to the team. The team has the responsibility to decide how much money to spend on salary, furniture, cars, whatever is needed for their business. Another example is to discuss and decide on performance and benefits for team members or disciplinary consequences.

Power to operative units

Operative units should implement strategic planning and strategic control functions. Only if an operative unit is incompetent should headquarters build functions. Headquarters acts as the "glue" of the organisation and is the strategic "playground." dm, a German drugstore, is one example for this approach. They delegate the responsibility for assortment, pricing and shop design to the subsidiary and with this they reduce levels of hierarchy.[30]

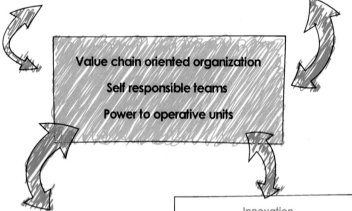

Speed

☐ Fast and flexible reaction to market
☐ Fast staffing, also cross divisional
☐ Fast restructuring without lots of
   bureaucracy and administration
☐ Less hierachy levels-less stumbling
   blocks
☐ Subsidiarity principle: HQ('s) only
   decides if unit is unable to decide
☐ Value chain and customer focused
   organization instead of tayloristic &
   functional divided organization

Flexibility

☐ Task rotation becomes easier
☐ Flexible employment of staff
   (cross divisional)
☐ Employees can be staffed more
   effective all over the conglomerate
☐ Mobility throught the company
   will be possible
☐ Format structure only for compliance reasons

Value chain oriented organization

Self responsible teams

Power to operative units

Culture

☐ Values and norms instead of rules
☐ Leadership through senses not
   hierarchy
☐ Control not by hiercharchy but team
   members
☐ High Level of self responsibility and
   self organization for individuals and
   teams
☐ Heterarchy instead of hierachy
   (decision making by the most
   competent employees

Innovation

☐ Task is not determined to one
   innovation department but
   becomes an inherent part of
   work for all units
☐ As units can manage their
   resources by themselves, they
   decide on their own which
   innovation to follow
☐ Less bureacracy means more
   energy and leeway for creativity,
   creation and innovation
☐ New form of collaboration:
   crowd sourcing, open innovation

Figure 3: Org 3.0 design principles and their influence on company challenges of the future organization.

Criteria for an Organisation's Survival

In our opinion, innovation, flexibility and speed, and culture are crucial and influential to an organisation's survival.

Innovation

Innovation is an inherent part of any job in Org 3.0. Some companies face major innovation problems, but in an Org 3.0 future, innovation can happen in every team or unit. Teams have the possibility and the responsibility to develop and implement ideas rapidly and directly, working as independent, autonomous units. These units budget and allocate resources to develop or optimise customer-oriented products and/or processes more quickly. They are directly responsible for the effects and results of their ideas. Innovation makes them simultaneously careful and effective.

In many of today's companies, management makes decisions and controls its accomplishments, requiring strict and widespread rules, instructions, and directives. The time this takes could be better invested in creativity, creation, and innovation.

Flexibility and speed

If units act along the value chain, connecting past functional boundaries, employees can be used more effectively and flexibly, and task rotation becomes easier.

Strengthening the operative units means accelerating reaction time to the market. Decision-making in large companies is normally hierarchical, meaning multiple management levels must concur. Following this hierarchical path up and down several lines causes long reaction times or, even worse, decisions being lost along the way. If units have a higher degree of freedom, their reaction time grows considerably faster.

Culture

Structure creates culture. An Org 3.0 structure creates an Org 3.0 culture. According to Niels Pfläging and Lars Vollmer, large companies usually function as "extrinsifiers," meaning that management assumes employees must be externally motivated and told which way to turn (Theory X). [31] An "intrinsifier" is a company with different perspective on its employees: management assumes its employees are intrinsically motivated, wish to deliver best results, and want to contribute to the company's successful future (Theory Y).

Perception of employees must change. We must be convinced as leaders that everyone is self-motivated, intrinsically self-motivated, and that they want to contribute and perform as well as possible - not because they are told to but because they want to. This perception allows delegation of responsibility to said employees. This perception is factually valid.

Org 3.0 implies a culture of trust and the willingness to let go of hierarchical power and control. Companies need to be sure of strategy alignment, but not necessarily through hierarchy. Control can be built by the whole team, or power can be given to leaders defined by competency, not hierarchy, enabling change if necessary. Decentralising decision competency implies the will to dispense with power at headquarters and entails a high degree of information transparency (e.g. budget plans), so that employees or teams can make the right decisions for the conglomerate.

Employees need to understand their contribution to and the influence of their work on the overall results. This mindset requires an understanding of the business's value creating process delivered by Org 3.0, and its information transparency and orientation on the value chain. All the energy going into bureaucracy and formalism can flow into value creation for customers and the company.

Generation Y and Org 3.0

Generation Y is used to direct communication, not communication via hierarchy. As discussed previously, they hold different values than Gen X or the Baby Boomers, and they want to direct the energy wasted in bureaucracy and hierarchy into value creation for the company and its customers. Org 3.0 will make less important a company's formal structure - and its hierarchy and power; the whole world of work will become more democratic, in great contrast to current working conditions. If formal structure is made less important, formal power's importance lessens as well, allowing employees more leeway in decision-making and action.

Leadership changes go hand-in-hand with Org 3.0. Leaders are coaches, not managers, working with self-responsible individuals and teams in a less hierarchical way, and changing their role to a more post-heroic one. It is possible and probable that these leaders will cede the power of decision making to employees more expert than they.

Our First Experiences with Org 3.0

As Change Mangers we noticed that one reorganisation quickly followed another. We found that the adjustment of the organisation structure did not keep up with reorganisations. We were very interested in organisations that were more flexible and less bureaucratic and looked at available literature, but realised that this topic is barely covered and only a few companies live some of aspects of Org 3.0. After developing our approach on a theoretical level, we sought out our first experience in real life, discussing our concepts with different functions and levels of employees and managers.

We learned that ceding power to operative units, and responsibility to teams, heightens team performance considerably. Leaders must act transparently, give orientation and coordinate work. They have to lead the team more like a moderator coordinating specialists. They are no longer the hero who makes decisions. The new way of leading is post-heroic. This leader holds responsibility with more leeway and less strict control than today's conventional leader. There was scepticism from existing management, because, perhaps, their role must change and, of course, means a loss of power for some.

This change is even more radical for expert managers (not leaders) who thought that the Org 3.0 system meant less internal managerial organisation. Org 3.0 is the opposite and managers need to understand that the new approach needs guidance, vision and a clear definition of expectations. Change leaders have to work very closely with managers, guiding them into the new system and teaching them to understand the new leadership style. Change managers must support the change process over time, as this goal cannot be achieved in one workshop.

On the other hand, we were hopeful that the organisation (managers and employees) could radically reduce bureaucracy and use faster, more professional decision-making processes.

To this end:

- We needed a sponsor at the highest level (CEO, whole board of management), for every change measure and for this entire radical approach.
- The new system works with "self regulation" but on the way to the new system we need organisation; for example setting up an assessment centre for management, and replacing

        managers with people with a much-needed post-heroic management style.

- Change leaders have to support the managers and employees in "building" their new organisation. They have a lot of questions, more even than we expected. The organisation has no experience with this new approach. Managers with courage are needed.
- There must be strict consequences if something heads in the wrong direction or managers do not align with the new management style.

"Org 3.0 islands" are the only way to begin implementing these concepts. Changing the entire company at once, particularly if it has thousands of employees or is globally distributed, is too complicated and expensive. The process is a journey, and change leaders must orchestrate and accompany. To our surprise, our approach turned out to be holistic, equalling the creation of a "new company."

Outlook and Next Steps

What do the organisational design principles of Org 3.0 and their implications on culture, reaction speed, flexibility, and innovation mean for the creation of a new organisational model?

BetaCodex proposes the "peach model," a hybrid organisation with central and peripheral elements. Cells close to the customer and to the market work autonomously, while the company headquarters is a strategic trigger and service unit. [32]

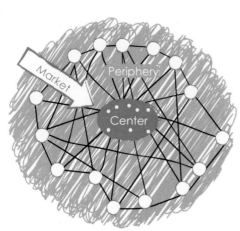

- Power to operative units: high level of self organization and responsibility

- Heterarchy: Decision making by most competent employees/teams

- Formal structure only for compliance reasons, focus on value creation structure

- Operative, decentralized units are formed by value crating chain

- Subsidiary principle: Head-quarters only decides if unit is unable to decide

- All functions (e.g.HR, F, audit,'H)   are implemented in operative units, only if a central service is better, it can be located in HQ

- Cells can react situational and autonomous

- Cultural/social control instead of hierachical

Based on Gerhard Wohland and Beta Codex

Figure 4: Hybrid, value oriented organization structure, according to Niels Pfläging

How can these cells be defined in large companies? Do we establish a large number of cells with every function (e.g. Human Resources) established in each cell? Does this sacrifice efficiency? Do we create value chains in different functions (e.g. product management), knowing the value chain does not end with one function? Do we ignore organisation models and allow cells to decide what the organisational design principles mean for them and their particular structure?

We take another step down the road of implementing Org 3.0 by asking:

> How do Org 3.0 islands and classical line units collaborate? How does the company cope in case of regression into line-model behaviour? How do we realise a sustainable Org 3.0?

We are currently running workshops of cross-divisional, cross-hierarchical, cross-functional participants to discuss these questions, and are attempting to find answers for them. Initial results confirm the organisational design principles outlined here. Our next step is to build a prototype of Org 3.0. After that we will discuss it with different departments and implement it. By implementing the new criteria in the department each units becomes an Org 3.0 island. The more Org 3.0 islands we can create, the bigger the impulse on the whole organisation will be.

Big Data and

Leadership

Start making sense

Mick Yates

Another Digital Day

First thing in the morning, we can download newspapers, check email, Facebook, Twitter, eBay, voicemail, phone calls. Which of these are in your morning digital routine?

Each digital activity creates data. What we do, where we "visit" - in bricks-and-mortar and digital worlds – what we see or buy is noted somewhere. Most data is collected by the websites visited or the services used.

Governments watch us too - they record what taxes are paid, our education, what cars are driven, what laws are adhered to, how passports are used, who is in the family circle, and our medical history.

At work, there's more email and the web. Depending on the company, customer data is collected – sales, credit histories, names, addresses, likes and dislikes. Internally, the company collects data on suppliers, manufacturing plants, process performance, and distribution systems. There is data on employee performance, salaries, and more.

Booking flights, hotel stays, or going to a restaurant creates more layers of data. During leisure time, millions of people stream music over the web, or upload pictures so that friends and family can see what they are doing and where they have been. Not just pictures are recorded - but also which friends view the pictures, their comments, where the photo was taken, and the camera settings used.

Beyond personal and business data, universities and scientists create terabytes of data, by watching stars, splitting the atom, testing new medicines, or studying social patterns.

Big Data is therefore everywhere. Until recently, it wasn't possible to aggregate and then interrogate unstructured data, like email and social media conversations, in conjunction with structured data, such as spread sheets and enterprise databases.

But now it's easier to combine these, using new technologies and algorithms. It's not only possible for industry, universities, and government – it is also becoming easier for individuals to collect and analyse all of their own data.

A Revolution – Big Data is Everywhere

The real issue is not the data itself – but what use we make of it, and what business and personal decisions it impacts. Never before have individuals had so much access to so much data – and making sense of it all is hard.

Professionally I've been dealing with customer insight data for a long time - I started my career in marketing at Procter & Gamble and continued in Johnson & Johnson where I was responsible for the Asia Pacific consumer business. Because leadership and change fascinate me, in 1997 I founded Leader-values.com, now one of the world's top leadership development websites. At the University of Leeds I teach Leadership Development in networked systems, with special interest in the human changes arising from the impact of "Big Data" and social media. Until recently, I was head of International Markets for Dunnhumby, a company that turns customer insight into business decisions.

First, we need to define "big data." In the 1990s, one example of Big Data was deriving useful insights from customer loyalty programmes to better communicate to and serve customers. Since then Big Data has exploded in the number of different sources and the ways in which it is connected. The need to generate useful insights and action is exactly the same, though, however big and complex the data set is.

IBM[1] suggested that Big Data spans four dimensions: volume, velocity, variety, and veracity.

- Volume: Enterprises are awash with ever-growing data of all types.
- Velocity: For time-sensitive processes such as fraud, Big Data must be used as it streams into the enterprise.
- Variety: Big Data is any type of data, structured and unstructured, such as text, sensor data, audio, video, click streams, and log files.
- Veracity: Many leaders don't trust the information they use to make decisions. Establishing trust in Big Data presents a huge challenge as the variety and number of sources grows. As ever, the data rule "garbage in, garbage out" is key.

While IBM suggests a strong technological framework, Gualteri[2] argued that Big Data has massive strategic and organisational implications for operating effectively, making decisions, reducing risks, and serving customers. Gualteri wrote we must store, process, and access. Can we capture and store the data? Can we cleanse, enrich, and analyse the data? Can we retrieve, search, integrate, and visualise the data?

The Economist[3] concluded that Big Data is a business game-changer. There is a strong link between financial performance and effective use of Big Data. Companies must have a well-defined data strategy in place before processing it, and must engage their managers across the business - always thinking about how data can improve performance.

However, as change leaders, we must help individuals and organisations become comfortable with the revolution that Big Data brings in their day-to-day work, and not just look at the technical and analytical aspects.

This chapter aims to be a Big Data primer for leaders and provides a practical outline of how we can use programmatic change models to help deal with the "human" side of the Big Data revolution.

Tiny Data + Unstructured Data = Big Data

I define "Tiny Data" as data from a single source in a structured format, which, while possibly a huge quantity, is limited in its complexity. The sheer number of terabytes is not really important nowadays, with our computing power. It is the combination of multiple data sources that makes things truly "Big." Even the databases held by major global enterprises, like credit card companies are, by this definition, "Tiny."

Unstructured data is exactly that – there is no fixed database format or coherent structure. Twitter messages, uploaded images, Facebook posts and likes, phone calls, customer service calls – all are unstructured data.

Big Data combines unstructured data and tiny data. My definition of Big Data is thus:

- Complex: Includes data sets from multiple sources and owners
- Combinatorial: Multiple "tiny" structured data sets and unstructured non-homogenous data
- Analysable: Needs new tools to capture, store, process, curate, analyse, and visualise it
- Useful: Creates decisive action plans by delivering insights within a tolerable elapsed time
- Pervasive: Impacts all organisational and people processes in the enterprise
- Personal: Provides individual access to data of all kinds

Technologies are now available that combine and make sense of these different sources – and most importantly, help turn the analytical results into useful insight and action.

For example, you might look at someone's Facebook timeline and note that they like wearing blue but never orange. If you are a clothing manufacturer and knew that fact, wouldn't that help you make more appropriate offers to that potential customer? And, personally, if you systematically knew people's colour preferences in this way, wouldn't you be able to buy them more appropriate presents?

This raises privacy issues, of course, yet there's another revolution going on – the move from business and government ownership of the data to individual access, and thus ownership.

Personal Ownership - An Individual Moment

Governments, companies, and universities collect all kinds of data, yet often an individual has to fight to access their own data; individuals create 70 percent of the data but enterprises are responsible for storing and managing 80 percent of it.[4]

This is shifting, as individuals are beginning to have personal access to all of their own data. Companies or government won't have the same broad access across all of the many data sources we generate.

Obvious privacy issues make it hard for even governments to aggregate disparate personal data sources (at least legally). Yet individuals will be able to analyse all of their own data, accessible via mobile devices and connected through the cloud, and create their own action plans from the insights. No longer will business or government have the monopoly on data and what to do with it.

Control, or at least the right to control, is shifting.

Industry has another challenge – trust. Would you let Facebook have your bank account details? Would you let your bank or Amazon have your emails to friends and family? That seems unlikely.

Even if individuals are not directly using some form of "aggregation app", all their data turns up on their locally controlled device, whether PC, Mac, tablet, or phone. Accounts are already connected in the social media sphere (login with Facebook or Twitter, anyone?), but now technology allows us to go much further.

Many companies are racing to create a secure "wallet" on our devices (Google, Apple, Square, credit card companies, and many others). In the first instance, these wallets will be for secure bank and shopping transactions. But when travel or restaurant details are added, movies and music included, your "chat" profile and what your friends like and do, the wallet will be a hugely powerful data source for analysis and predictions of all kinds.

At its crudest implementation, knowing a little more about individual preferences and likes can lead to more targeted and therefore more effective advertising. That's what Google does. But it also gives us, the individual, a better understanding of the value of our own data.

We are entering a data marketplace. Individuals create and increasingly access all of their own data, and government and business want it. An exchange will take place. Individuals will want something of value in return for access to their data.

Pre-Big Data, businesses offered loyalty programmes in exchange for customer purchase data. The currency of exchange was rewards, gifts, miles, and cash back. Today, when the individual has the data, the cash exchange will go the other way.

With ever increasing demands from customers and dramatic advances in technology, business has no choice but to learn how to understand and then effectively work with this change in data control.

Change leaders must understand both the enterprise and personal implications of Big Data if we are to help deal with these revolutions.

In my work, I have used a leadership framework researched at Oxford and HEC as part of my Master's programme to practically organise how to approach this challenge as programmatic change.

A Big Data Action Plan

My focus is organisational and people change, not technology. The words "enterprise" and "business" are used interchangeably, as are "consumer" and "customer". "Client" is used to reference business-to-business, as I am focused on commercial rather than government implications.

The framework for the programmatic change plan is the 4E's, beginning as a top-down process. First, my leadership definition:

Leadership is the energetic process of getting other people fully and willingly committed to a new course of action, to meet commonly agreed objectives while holding common values.

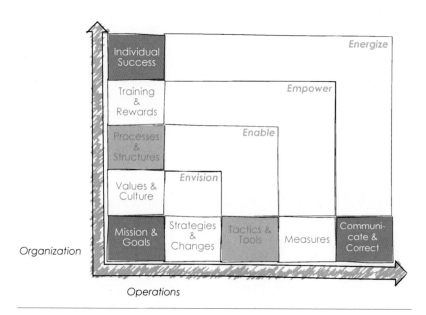

Figure 3: The 4Es Framework

This has two dimensions – organisational (people) and operational (task) - and is a sequential leadership process:

- *Envision* the future, using the vast array of insights available from Big Data.
- *Enable* the enterprise, with strategies, technologies and systems to create action on this insight.

- *Empower* individuals, to organise effectively, to innovate, deliver results and drive value.
- *Energise* everyone in the team consistently and constantly, and course correct as needed.

The framework is focused on "actions in use" rather than "espoused" or claimed competencies, individual styles, or personality types. It therefore defines a practical process. Let's apply it to the Big Data revolution by first examining some macro-themes.

Johnson & Johnson: Global and De-centralised

Whilst Company Group Chairman in Asia Pacific, we needed to maintain local customer knowledge but do a better job of spreading best practice to speed the flow of ideas across the region. Why were we changing? I offered:

> Currently, if you have a business issue that you cannot resolve, you pass it up the line – to your boss and the country manager.

> In the new world, you will know someone in another country – maybe in another discipline – that can help you solve the problem. You will then be able to present solutions to your boss, not problems.

> This gives you the chance to innovate and solve problems – owning your own business - rather than being told what to do.

The change was successful. Today, moving best practices around like this is a fundamental of business. Technology can help drive this, and data can inform success, but it needs to be rooted in clear strategies. In my research, two strategic dynamics are entwined with Big Data.

- Customer Centricity – Big Data Style
- Innovation in a Network

The change challenge is then the integration and blending of these two strategies along with the dynamics of programmatic change.

Customer Centricity – Big Data Style

First, the transition of data ownership to the individual and increasing customer power suggests that the most important response to Big Data is to embrace customer centricity. The Customer truly is in charge.

Customer and client interactions are moving from "push" strategies to "pull" (Hagel[5] Siegel [6]). Instead of businesses "pushing" services and products at customers, the individual can now discriminate and "pull" services to them – to suit their exact needs, preferences, and timing.

Big Data makes this ever more practicable. Think of Amazon and its "other customers also bought" feature. Individuals view other customers' recommendations, access the products and services that they need, and optimise how it is delivered and how it is used.

Customer centricity is about meeting all customer needs, and using data-driven insights to build effective customer programmes is critical. This requires everyone in the enterprise to change his or her mind-set.

In the 1990's, Kroger, now the USA's second largest retailer, was losing the battle to Wal-Mart. They decided to focus on delivering what customers really wanted, and adopted a "Customer 1st" programme. All Kroger employees were educated on the strategy shift and implications, and trained on better serving customers. Kroger has shown consistent sales growth every quarter since 2003 - even through the 2008-2012 recessionary periods. The customer rewarded Kroger's strategic focus.

In my experience, there are several steps needed to create a successful customer centric approach.

A. Offer a fair exchange for the customer's data

Customers are used to getting value from loyalty programmes. In the most successful cases, redemption rates on targeted offers are extremely high - customers like getting cash back on purchases. The customer believes that they are getting consistent value from the exchange; otherwise they would give up the loyalty programme.

As more data types are included, the data has even more value than "simple" purchase records. Businesses need to offer more than promotions. Possible approaches include:

1) Helping the customer make sense of all of their data with analytics

2) Multi-business partnerships to broaden returns and rewards from data exchange

3) Connecting together the customer experience at every touch point with the business to make things easier for the customer

4) Ever more personalised products and services (see 'B' below), and 5) even paying the customer for their data.

The mind-set shift is from "We own it to profit from it" to "We curate it to create value for you, the customer."

B. Personalise the offer, service, or product

Today, everything is becoming increasingly personalised, and the traditional mass market is dwindling. Data based methods are really important to help customers navigate this personalisation.

Amazon identifies books and other items that customers might like based on previous purchases ("If you liked that, you might like this"). iTunes matches music tastes with suggested "genius playlists."

UK Tesco is another good example. Every 3 months, millions of direct mail offers are sent to their customers. Virtually all have a unique combination of product and promotional offers, as well as a cash "reward" for past purchases made. After all, there is no point sending a dog food offer to someone who only has cats!

All are effective but relatively simple examples of personalised offers based on prior purchases by customers. Now, multiple data sets can be combined to provide a more comprehensive view of customer behaviour. If a business knew what restaurants you like, or vacation places you go, they could suggest new books, music, or other products which couldn't be predicted based merely on your past purchases.

Glimpsing into the future, 3D printing is coming. We will be able to order unique items "on demand." Imagine a shoe store that can create an exact fit in an infinite range of styles and colours. Imagine the customer viewing the shoes against the database of her own wardrobe. Imagine checking what friends and others have created or tried, to be sure it is the perfect choice. Combining different data sources will be key to this "extreme" personalisation.

Technology encourages such "mass personalisation." With this comes a mind-set change from "This is how we do it" to "This is what you've asked for." Ford's comment about the Model T - "You can have it in any colour you want providing it is black" - is as dated as the Model T itself.

C. Engage customers to positively advocate your products and *services*

According to Forrester Research[7], more than 60 percent of consumers interact with brands in multiple channels. As they shop in-store, browse for recipes on their phone, view catalogues on their iPad, look for input from other consumers in online forums, and ask questions via Twitter, it is increasingly difficult to distinguish between traditional shopping and communication or marketing channels.

Customer mind-sets are shifting to an integrated view of their universe, regardless of device. As individual customers share their views, likes, and ideas, "social curation" shares these at zero cost.

"Crowd distribution" of advertising is essentially free. As an example of a brand making good use of this, Palmolive ran a social advocacy "word of mouth" campaign. They gained good recognition for the absence of unnecessary chemicals or heavy fragrances in the "Pure and Clear" campaign – and they drove sales.

7,500 Agents participated (via BzzAgent[8], a US subsidiary of dunnhumby). With product information activities, samples, coupons, and social media, the campaign reached over 430,000 people, and over 75,000 purchases were made.

Then consider the power of instant news disseminated by Twitter and news aggregators like Zite. Users define the news that is really important to them, not the traditional broadcasters. We pick and chose what to read and what to share, influencing how our friends view the world. At each step, as we converse, curate and share that news, Big Data sets are forming and being used.

We listen to what friends say about products, brands, and services. We take notice of what people write about books and music on Amazon. "Voting" on products is everywhere and we happily give vendor feedback on the likes of eBay and Amazon increasing capacity for collaborative design.

The mind-set shift is for business to "converse and collaborate."

Innovation is a Network

Long gone are the days of a single genius creating everything. Edison was indeed a genius – but even he had a research lab. These days, networks help businesses innovate and take advantage of Big Data. These networks speed the flow of new ideas, best practices, products, and services across functions and across geographies.

Historically, innovation came from internal Research & Development groups (R&D), yet ideas can come from anywhere – suppliers, customers, universities and government. Networks are powerful innovation tools.

When Procter & Gamble's "Connect & Develop" programmes opened R&D to external networks, results were astounding: according to a Harvard Business Review study[9], R&D productivity increased by nearly 60 percent. Externally created innovations comprised 35 percent of new products (up from 15 percent), and 45 percent of total product development initiatives.

Innovate to enable network operations

Technology begins with database design made "fit for analytical purpose." This includes the right data capture systems, storage, processing, and access (Gualteri), and it impacts the entire business.

According to Gartner[10], by 2017 Chief Marketing Officers (CMOs) will outspend Chief Information Officers (CIOs) on data and analytics. If CMOs and CIOs develop big data strategies in silos, a seamless customer experience will be impossible. Technology enables change, but it is the human being that creates insight, conversation, service, and action. The possibilities for innovation in service delivery within network operations are significant. So is the potential for disjointed results.

Delegating big data strategies to the CIO or the CMO without an overall business data strategy across the networked organisation may waste the investment and miss opportunities.

Innovate in the right kind of analytics

Literature is awash with talk about Customer Relationship Management (CRM) tools. Usually CRM focuses on customer contact and communication, but it does not automatically drive new insights and action. Nor do CRM systems allow constructive two-way involvement with customers. Too often CRM systems are about "push" strategies and handling complaints. Leaders who depend solely on CRM miss the opportunity of two-way interaction with customers.

Innovate in a common language

Businesses need a common customer language across their organisations, and need to share this with suppliers and other third parties. A connected internal and external network is of no value if different language is used in different parts of the network. Precious resources waste time reconciling definitions and fixing errors in data definitions, calculations and resulting interpretation of meaning.

Mapping and aligning the use of terms, language and definitions across the extended network of the organisation, its customers and suppliers is major change effort – and the leader's focus on the right language is a daily discipline necessary for success.

Innovate with external networks

Innovation networks drive new product ideas and execution. Online exchanges between "seekers" and "finders" are now everywhere, expanding the group creating ideas, and dramatically lowering cost.

Research (Harvard Business Review [11]) has shown that a large number of novel ideas come from "solvers" working outside the fields normally expected by the "seekers." In other words, new knowledge is coming from unexpected quarters, including customers. Technology, connectivity, rapid data flows and analysis are the keys to success. Open source must be the organisational paradigm. The mind-set shifts from "invented here = right," to "invented anywhere = best."

Engage individual customers in co-creation of products and services

Digital growth and data explosion provide opportunities to gather broader, timelier, and more actionable feedback, to prompt customers to co-design and innovate products and services.

Indian multinational Tata Group's Tanishq invites customers to co-create jewellery. Ideas submitted reveal insights on the collection, and identify intelligent, creative, and smart young designers with great ideas.

Full co-creation of products with customers is in its infancy but firms as disparate as Coca Cola, MTV, E.ON, and Heineken are exploring the possibilities. Coca Cola encourages customers to add to its creative stock by telling stories about events at which its product is drunk, while Heineken runs a design contest for its consumers to create a "unique club experience."

In these examples, the business works cooperatively in social systems with customers to identify new ideas. Feedback loops iterate and improve the ideas, and the data created is used to manage everything for best results.

Applying the 4E's in Big Data

Applying the 4 E's in phases of planned programmatic change.

ENVISION an Enterprise that is Customer Centric and Uses Innovation Networks

Most change practitioners will be familiar with programmatic change. The 4E's align change activity in 11 sequential steps. Here I focus on big data questions, entwined with the imperatives of customer centricity and innovation networks.

1. Create a clear case for change that inspires people

There are three questions for leaders to consider:

1. What are the strategic implications for business and the personal implication of Big Data ownership and the upcoming value exchange to your business?

2. Consider the operational challenges. Do existing strategic choices in the business help or hinder the use of Big Data?

3. From an organisational viewpoint, consider the value system of the enterprise. Are your organisation's current values conducive to the world of Big Data, or do they need adjustment?

Getting everyone in the business to understand the differences between the current state and the Big Data future state is essential in an effective change programme.

2. Create and describe a viable vision of an alternative and successful state which touches each individual in the organisation

In other words, what will the "case for change" mean in practical terms?

ENABLE a Big Data Business

Change leaders create enabling conditions for the organisation to succeed. What follows does not focus on the obvious need for the right technologies. Rather, it prioritises organisational and "people" issues.

3. Put change agents in place with a guiding coalition of willing leaders

Teams are fundamentally important to the success of the programme. No one person can develop the right vision, eliminate all obstacles to success, lead dozens of subsidiary change projects, create quick wins en route, write all necessary processes, and shift an organisation's culture.

Who is best placed (attitudes, skills, and influence) to co-lead the change? Is the pipeline of talent ready for Big Data? Big Data is creating a major talent gap in most organisations. In a recent Economist[12] survey, 41 percent of top managers said their organisations did not have the skills to deal with Big Data.

4. Consistently drive the change from the top of the enterprise

Without top-level leadership nothing will happen. Change leaders must not only stay the course, but also ensure that their "guiding coalition" does, too. Do you as a leader have the discipline and the will to see this through? To quote Kotter [15]:

> *Guaranteed to Fail: The problem in failed change initiatives is rarely that the case for change is poorly thought out, or not supported with sufficient facts. A solid business case that has a theoretically "compelling" rationale only appeals to people's head and not their heart.*

> *Guaranteed to Succeed: Leaders who know what they are doing will "aim for the heart." They will connect to the deepest values of their people and inspire them to greatness. They will make the business case come alive with human experience, engage the senses, create messages that are simple and imaginative, and call people to aspire.*

It is necessary to "be the change" (as Gandhi said) and to do so with consistent and constant messaging. Bring alive to people the reality of the new world of Big Data, customers, and networks.

5. Set a realistic scale and pace of change with a clear sense of urgency

Most change programmes start with a great sense of urgency from enterprise leaders. There is often a "burning platform", a major business problem to fix.

Yet, Kotter research in 1995, and again later from McKinsey[13], 70 percent of all major change management programmes fail. Many are late and over-spend. There are several reasons for this, although in my own experience, having unrealistic expectations is a critical factor.

I was responsible for J&J's Asia Pacific consumer business in the 1990s, when we decided to install regional SAP financial and operational systems, rather than rely on legacy systems that varied by country. The value of SAP is the consistency and quality of data it produces, and thus the decision making it facilitates. In the end, this project helped the business, but it exceeded budget and was many months late. What went wrong?

First, we underestimated the time needed to remap current business processes to SAP processes. Secondly, the schedule was too tight – when one thing slipped behind, everything slipped. Third, we needed a more realistic assessment of training needs. Expectations were mismatched with reality.

The moral of the story? Every change project must balance the need for realism with the need for urgency. Once implemented, Big Data can dramatically improve transparency inside the enterprise, can drive down execution times and underpin organisational urgency. Pragmatically this is possible when systems are the same and data is mapped correctly. Then transparency and faster execution can occur.

6. Create an integrated transition programme, from the current state to the desired future

The objective of a step-wise transition plan is that everyone embraces it. In the J&J SAP example, we initially had a lacklustre integration programme.

Have you got a clear road map from pre- to post- Big Data, customer and networked states? How are you enabling and embracing everyone in the organisation?

Insights from Big Data can inform existing decision processes across the business, adding a new lens. For example, all retailers have ways they set prices. Big Data can give better insight on how customers view and act on pricing, so that the business can create an alternate plan, which can be tested and validated in-store.

Feedback loops can help fix problems and adapt plans as things move forward. Insights from Big Data can help leaders continually assess progress. In effect, measurement allows the enterprise to close the loop on action planning and course correction.

> 7. Create a unique organisation shape to show how tasks and people fit the new world

"Every organisation is perfectly designed to gets the results that it gets," Dave Hannah[14] wrote when describing high performance work systems.

The corollary is that any existing enterprise will have to exert energy to change, and some will have a hard time morphing into a business successfully using Big Data.

Are you and your leadership willing to develop alternate organisation structures? Are you able to make these pre-eminent? New multi-functional project teams, outside of the hierarchy, may be the best way to execute change.

EMPOWER Everyone to Think and Act Big Data

> 8. Execute a symbolic end to the status quo

Having a clear and visible end to the "old" while also dealing with change can be very powerful.

What elements of your culture do you need to preserve? What needs to change? What will demonstrate this change?

Here is an example not to follow: Al Dunlap was hired to turn around Scott Paper. The same day that he took over as CEO, he invested $2 million of his own money into the business to show his confidence that the company could be changed. On his first day, Dunlap offered three of his former associates top jobs in the company. On the second day he disbanded the powerful management committee. On the third day he fired nine of the eleven highest-ranking executives. On the fourth day he destroyed four bookshelves crammed with strategic plans of previous administrations.

While this "slash and burn" approach did dramatically improve profits in the first year, it lost customers, killed company culture, and destroyed employee loyalty. Essentially Dunlap was saying that everything before his tenure at Scott was bad, and he had a lock on the truth.

A better example to follow: Lou Gerstner successfully turned around IBM by shifting the focus from products and big machines to client services – and he cut costs and reduced the workforce. The change succeeded. Gerstner spent time ensuring that all employees and customers understood the change. IBM remains a powerful business today.

Gerstner was criticised at the time for being "slow" but the process was respectful of the company's history and culture, while very clear on the goals. Gerstner succeeded in building trust while creating a sustainable culture change, where Dunlap didn't.

Empowerment is about building sustainable trust and interdependence, with people working together for a common set of objectives, and culture is key. Understanding the current culture (through paradigms, rituals, stories, and routines, among others) allows the design of effective interventions.

A technique that I use is Appreciative Inquiry (AI). This gets individuals to participate in the change process, rather than just be passive observers.

AI is a cycle that goes from "discovering the best of what is", via "imagining what could be" to "designing what it should be" to "creating what it is".

AI discovers the good things already going on in the enterprise, and builds on them. The process encourages people to dream about the conditions for success, and how to codify, magnify and make them happen.

9. Build options and plans to deal with likely resistance

Most people fear change to one degree or another, which can lead to outright resistance to the change. Understanding the nature of this resistance is vital. People are concerned about not having the skills or experience to do new work. However other issues are usually more important to them – for example, being out of work and not being able to support the family, or losing respect and position in the company. All combine to create anxiety and possibly outright resistance.

Consider external implications: customers are used to a certain way of things happening. A friend told me recently about changes at his bank. Currently, he has a premium account, reflecting long-standing loyalty to the bank. The bank is in the process of splitting into two separate parts, to create more "shareholder value" and my friend has been told a) he has no choice but to continue to do business with one part of the bank chosen for him and b) that means he becomes a regular customer, no longer premium. Do you think he will stay with that bank or switch?

Change leaders need to move decisively on real blockages to change, including removing individuals from the organisation if necessary. However, the most effective leaders create a picture of a positive future and build a sustainable culture that nurtures the change to Big Data, without engendering a negative culture of fear. They spend time ensuring individual customers understand what's happening, why they should both stick with the organisation, and perhaps even ask the customer to help make the change happen.

Of course there might still be resistance, and the change leader must be aware, acting accordingly. Dealing with resistance by understanding what is good, and only act on the negative as a last resort. Involve your customers in the change from the beginning.

ENERGISE Everyone by Becoming a Big Data Leader

10. Constantly advocate the change – course correct on problems and maintain momentum

Usama Fayyad is the founder of ChoozOn, a business that helps individual customers decide between competing offers. Working with many companies on their most challenging (Big) data analysis problems, Fayyad concludes:

> The real challenge is one of Leadership. The technology provides the raw material. The art puts that raw material to good use. But Leadership is what puts it on the agenda so action can be taken.

Are you, the leader, prepared to show up day after day as the Big Data Leader? Are you prepared and able to change metrics and rewards to support your Big Data programme?

The leader's personal commitment to the change must be communicated in all media – traditional, social, and face-to-face. Face-to-face interaction is where the leader's message can really come alive.

> *11. Create a locally owned rewards plan, so everyone benefits from the change*

A locally owned rewards plan ensures that everyone benefits from the change. For example, some companies base a large percentage of senior management bonuses on meeting customer Key Performance Indicators (KPIs), in addition to more traditional profit and sales targets. You get what you measure and reward.

Leading in Times of Big Data

Our everyday lives are no longer solely built on interpersonal connections and choices. Every aspect of our digital day creates data, amassing an unprecedented footprint that weaves into our professional, social, and personal experiences.

Any leader must consider the impact of the Big Data revolution – both for business decision making and personal "control" of our own data – and make it a priority.

Technology is just beginning to let us capture this wealth of customer insight, analyse it, and turn it to good purpose. But the shifting axis of power means that we will simultaneously rely more and more on the trust and cooperation of individuals who want to control their data identity.

Even a glance at the recent revelations that the US and UK governments gathered citizen data without consent reveals the growing wariness of those who want to study our digital selves.

Businesses need to offer a fair exchange for access and use of this data, but businesses must accept that they are no longer in control; tmikhe individual is.

Enterprise-wide focus on customer centricity, deep analytics, and consequent insights can drive decisions in all parts of the business. Internal and external innovation networks will further drive new ideas in the business.

The principles and processes of programmatic change are time honoured. Build on shared values; envision the future; enable with tools, technologies, and appropriate organisation structures; empower employees to act, build trust and interdependence; energise the entire system by "walking the talk" and asking the right questions.

The leader's role in the era of Big Data is as important as ever.

Straight Lines Won't Get You There

Unlocking the Digital Mind

John O'Loan

Every morning, two huge trucks arrive at the UK Government's vehicle licensing authority in Wales, where before lunch an army of staff unloads cages of letters, files, forms, and paperwork. This is sorted into smaller bundles and labelled, and then sorted into smaller bundles and labelled again. After that, even smaller, labelled bundles are delivered to desks all over the building.

After lunch, another army of less mobile workers analyse, cross check, rubber stamp, and repackage those smaller bundles, then sorts them into bigger bundles and re-label again. By late afternoon bundles are loaded back into the two massive trucks. This has been the method for 110 years since automobile licenses were issued in the UK.

Basically this also how a computer works on the Internet. Digital networking is quicker - not just because physical bundling takes time and manpower, but also because those bundles need to be transported from A to B and then back again.

Today we have something cleverer. Digital is speed. Analogue is bureaucracy. Digital is the enemy of bureaucracy. Today things happen in "a cloud" of lightening fast, interconnected nodes of intelligence.

Human society is characterised by similar physical analogous processes - our work, commerce, and leisure. Analogue is so 'second nature', we believed it was 'human nature'.

So, while we can use digital networking as a tool, it won't actually change us will it? You can't change human behaviour, can you? Well, yes of course you can. Change leadership requires understanding that change is necessary and then sets a path to achieve that change.

Analogue is passé

The old kind of linear, analogue thinking processes can't explain, understand or compete, in a digitally networked world - any more than the Wright brothers could have flown to the moon.

Many of our time honoured institutions are battered by digital driven changes and are failing. Media, politics, finance, education, health, and cities don't understand, can't keep up, or simply can't change.

I grew up in an analogue world, where everything in daily life went from A to B to C to D, like the vehicle licensing authority mail, without much thought or opportunity for doing things differently. Complexity was handled in small steps. But to survive in today's more complex world we need to think differently, because previous processes are a product of a different analogue environment, no longer valid or adequate in a world run by networked intelligence.

It's hard to point to any other social or industrial influence which has so deeply and quickly effected such dramatic change across the globe, than networked digitisation. It affects not just the way our media and information is distributed, but like a four year old with an iPad, also the way we are learning to think.

For this we can thank the Google algorithm. It has saved us from descending into worldwide chaos, from drowning in a sea of knowledge. It is the very antithesis of linear thinking. It is pure, digitised, networked thought, and the world will never be the same again. We now have a tool that takes all our thoughts and looks at them as a network, via links. Watching the algorithm operate in real time would look chaotic, but the result is coherent – and vital.

Unlike the 'start to finish' concentration required of the human mind in the past, online reading encourages the brain to jump across thoughts and references, teaching the brain new skills.

The War of Two Worlds

British science fiction writer, social reformer, biologist, and historian H.G. Wells wrote a number of essays and delivered several lectures in the years leading up to the Second World War in which he described his vision for a *World Brain*, which he was sure could bring world peace.[1]

Its basis was to be a new, free, synthetic, authoritative and permanent World Encyclopaedia. He looked to technology to provide it, so that "any student, in any part of the world" would be able to "examine any book, any document, in an exact replica." This he hoped would produce world peace through "a common understanding and the conception of a common purpose and of a commonwealth such as now we hardly dream."

His main concern at the time was for assimilation of that information and its distribution, realising that "our contemporary encyclopaedias are still in the coach and horses days, rather than in the phase of the automobile and the aeroplane." In the search for such a facility, we seem to have caught up with Wells' vision, but what unforeseen effects could it have?

Maryanne Wolf is a professor of child development, and the Director of the Centre for Reading and Language Research at Tufts University, Boston, MA. Her work on dyslexia led her to trace the development of the reading brain through early human history. She believes, according to her research[2], that the human brain was not originally wired to read. Reading is an acquired skill, the basis of which is learned primarily in early childhood, along with the ways we think, communicate and express our thoughts.

Is it possible to 'change' the way we 'think', if our previous communication and thinking habits are not hard wired? Father Walter Jackson Ong, an American Jesuit priest, professor of English Literature at St Louis University in the United States, historian and philosopher, showed through his research[3] that the brain sees writing as a technology, like any other technology, which when introduced into a new culture has wide-ranging effect on all areas of life. Writing transforms the basis of what was previously known in the brain, much as any new technology would do. Cultures without previous access to, or knowledge of, writing technology would require alternate strategies to preserve their important information, such as song, dance and storytelling.

After introduction of a new technology (such as writing), Dr. Ong found the brain adapts. The previous strategies, created in the absence of the new technology, are no longer used and subsequently 'forgotten'. A young Canadian named Marshall McLuhan supervised Father Ong's thesis at St Louis University - he would later become the media guru who coined the mantra "The Medium Is the Message."

At the height of the 'analogue glory days' of Westernised media development (1960s and 70s), McLuhan's ideas fuelled many of the changes in media and advertising. By the time of his death in 1980 he'd reversed his mantra to "The Message is the Medium", claiming it worked either way. With that contradiction, his influence began to wane. Today in the digital age the message from the man who foresaw the Internet 25 years out has never been clearer.

Digital Minds

With changes in media and information distribution forced by digital technology came some of the biggest social, organisational, and cultural upheavals in modern history.

When the family unit was breaking down, family members ('demographic units') would separate themselves into their own rooms to immerse themselves into their own interests derived from various media. New research by Britain's media regulator Ofcom shows that family members are now starting to congregate together again, even if still engrossed in their own media interests. Ofcom believes that while human nature hasn't changed – we like to congregate together – digital media is now portable, making it possible for people to bring their own interests with them.

H.G. Wells, among others, saw the need for digitalisation, and the benefits it could provide. Researchers like Wolf and Ong assure us that the brain can cope and adapt to a new language and a new way of thinking. Guru Marshal McLuhan foresaw that the processing of information would become at least as, if not more, important than the actual content provided.

McLuhan asserted that whenever a new medium is introduced (or in Ong's case, any new 'technology'), people will at first be more interested in the content it carries, the stories it tells, than the technology itself. He believed that media channels do not just carry information; they also shape our thought process. McLuhan went further, stating that "the effects of technology do not occur at the level of opinions or concepts" but on the physical nervous system itself. Content, he said, is just "the juicy piece of meat carried by the burglar, to distract the watchdog of the mind." [4]

Most of McLuhan's research was based on what we call today 'lean back media'. The term describes an information flow in which the consumer/audience sits across the room and simply watches/observes/ listens to (passively) the electronic media or information from the written page. How much more consuming - and transforming - can the interactive 'lean forward media' be, since it requires a greater level of active engagement? Could Wells and McLuhan have envisaged its full effect?

The director of Novak Druce Centre for Professional Service Firms, Reader and Fellow of Oxford, Chris McKenna is well qualified to point to lessons for the change leader from the two past Industrial Revolutions to the Third Industrial Revolution he sees happening now.

While it's tempting to see recent technical revolutions as unprecedented, interesting parallels and strategic lessons can be drawn from previous attempts at building technological systems and business models.

At a Saïd Business School conference in 2012 McKenna told his audience that while the First Industrial Revolution was spurred by the deployment of more rapid, economical, and widespread transport, following Stevenson's rocket steam train, the Second Industrial Revolution was the result of continuous production, which led to mass production.[5]

With so many goods to move, marketing those products became as important as price and was built on strong product and corporate branding. 'Positioning' is part of branding, which is why every Rolls Royce came with its own driver.

Kodak's breakthrough wasn't the Box Brownie camera itself, but the new convenience of film on a roll. General Electric built massive power stations, to replace the furnaces for modern conveyor belt production, but their vast capacity was unused at night. To use more capacity than just electric lights, new technologies such as radios, toasters, washing machines, irons, and vacuum cleaners were pushed into the shops.

Eventually this led to precision engineering, product and procedure standardisation, and a kind of 'lock in', some of which is still with us a century later.

Lock In

The first typewriters were invented by The Reverend Rasmus Malling-Hansen in 1865, to aid deaf and mute members of a Copenhagen institute. His first models, and then the golden writing ball device he later perfected, had one problem – the device covered the paper, so the typist couldn't be sure of what was on the page until the typing was finished. They also found the best layout for its 52 individual keys, as did Christopher Latham Sholes, a newspaper editor and printer from Milwaukee. The problem with the 'upright' typewriters in the United States and Britain was that the keys jammed as they moved to strike the page and the typist couldn't see the printed page behind the mangle of arms and letter 'shoes'. Sholes devised a 'jam proof' keyboard layout and sold it to Remington, about the time Malling-Hansen began marketing its Golden Ball blind typewriter. Remington changed Sholes' original layout, mainly by replacing the key designed for the full stop with the letter "R". The "QWERTY" keyboard was born.

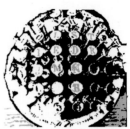

top-view

Figure 1: The Hansen Writing Ball, the first commercially produced typewriter. The pincushion-like Hansen Writing Ball was invented in 1865 by Rasmusv Malling-Hansen, the principal of the Royal Institute for the deaf-mutes in Copenhagen. It was first patented and entered production in 1870.

Whatever the reason for the change, the same QWERTY layout designed in the late 1800s to avoid key jam and to sell typewriters is still in use today on our laptops - when we have no keys and sell no typewriters – it is 'locked in'.

We don't use the Golden Ball today because its application did not fit its time and technology. If it were not for the intervening technology and "locked in", applications retained as a legacy of now out-dated technology, the one handed keypad could well be improving speed and technology, today.

It's just one example of successive generations going along with the same old thinking, even if there's no further need for it, even if new thinking could produce an improvement like the Golden Ball keyboard.

As Alexander Graham Bell discovered in the United States, lock in and the 'network' effect can work together to develop strong sales potential: more telephones installed means more devices in use, so more telephones are sold, but the more 'standard' (locked in) a system becomes, the more it resists change.

Red and green traffic lights are an example of lock in. In Western culture, red is synonymous with danger, so it was chosen as the Stop colour on traffic lights. Green for go and red for stop is 'locked in' all over the world. In China red is a symbol of good fortune and in India it's the colour for matrimony. In the past China changed their traffic light system so that red, the colour most associated with the Communist Party, would be seen as synonymous with progress (go) rather than stop (green), but the resulting chaos made Beijing realise that some things are beyond easily 'unlocking' without disastrous consequences.

The concepts of 'lock in' and 'networking' remain important in our digital, non-linear world. Even though they helped shape our previous, analogue, society, they (and the ideas of Wells) help explain where we are today. They give us greater assurance that in Einstein's words, "To change the world, we must change our thinking" - and that if we do, it will work.

Recognising lock in and network effect for what they are, and dealing with them as forces to resist change, is the first step required for a change leader to remove road blocks in clients' understanding that change is necessary.

Tim Berners-Lee was reared by parents who could see change (they helped develop the first commercially built computer, the Ferranti Mark 1). He grew up in the McLuhan Guru era, was an avid science fiction reader and a fan of H.G. Wells. He graduated from Oxford with a first class degree in Physics. Then he worked for Plessey telecommunications, creating typesetting software for printers.

His first research projects for Plessey concerned networked transactional systems, multi-skilling, and intelligent typesetting. In March 1989, this man would write the basic outline for the idea that became the World Wide Web. Entitled simply "Information Management: A Proposal," his paper convinced the CERN Institute in Switzerland to allow him to move from his 'abstract' to a practical demonstration. He linked a Hypertext Transfer Protocol (HTTP) client and server via the Internet just eight months later. The world would never be the same.

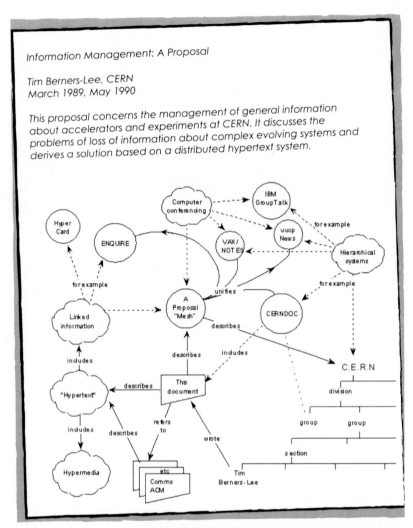

Information Management: A Proposal

Tim Berners-Lee, CERN
March 1989, May 1990

This proposal concerns the management of general information about accelerators and experiments at CERN. It discusses the problems of loss of information about complex evolving systems and derives a solution based on a distributed hypertext system.

Source: CERN (Conseil Europeen pour la Recherche Nucleaire)

Figure 2: The internet as proposed

At the same time, the 'satellite revolution' started to overtake earth-bound communication, creating "an unambiguous threat" to the old world order.[6] *Networking* was speeding up - and that didn't just mean speed dating at drinks parties.

Convergence

10 years later - while people were still wondering where to put the tollbooth on the digital super highway - something even more profound happened.

Interconnecting one type of media to another (for example, print to sound or video to print) has been limited by the specifically different form in which they were created - one television system couldn't "talk to" another, a cylinder recording couldn't play a phonograph, and a Betamax wouldn't play in a VHS machine.

Analogue (Adjective):

An analogue device uses some type of information to measure, process or control another variable that is fundamentally different in nature.

For example, a vinyl record uses a varying groove which can create a mechanical displacement of the phonograph needle or stylus that corresponds with the frequency and amplitude of sounds.

Similarly, magnetic video and audio tape recorders use varying magnetic signals, analogous with sound and images. Analogue signals are continuous.

In contrast, digital equipment uses binary signals, meaning a combination of either presence or absence of charge, north or south polar magnetisation, a hole or no hole at a given location in a punched card or some other either-or signal. Binary signals are discrete.

Because books are "analogue" to the mind, they require concentration. They don't offer their own distractions (except if you cheat the author and leap forward) and a book keeps you in a predetermined environment. The brain needs to make connections, requiring additional, complicated, and often physical manipulation of the individual medium.

While the brain has, to varying degrees, developed the power of lateral thinking, the media we use to enrich and extend our thinking remain largely linear or analogue. Those differences create barriers to their distribution. While those barriers were sometimes overcome, usually by technological translation, the process remained analogue - A to B, a straight line. Once media is digitised, there are few boundaries, other than interconnectivity. Once the Net and web provide that interconnectivity, there are no boundaries.

Rebuilding the World ...

in the Age of Networked Intelligence

Dan Tapscott of nGenera sees a crisis of leadership left in the wake of this algorithm-lead revolution: "Paradigm shifts involve dislocation, conflict, confusion and uncertainty. New paradigms are nearly always received with coolness, even mockery or hostility. Those with vested interests such as investments in money, time and understanding, are the first to fight the change. They may also be too old to want to change. The shift demands such a different view that established leaders often are the last to be won over, if at all."[7]

In an earlier study (2008) Tapscott found that digital immersion had a profound effect on the way younger adapters, those who had grown up using the World Wide Web, absorbed information. Instead of reading a page from top to bottom, left to right, it was normal to 'skip and scan' down the page, looking for words of interest, rather than following thoughts down the page, linearly. While similar to speed reading of old, the addition of embedded links, whatever thought process the author was attempting to guide the reader on is gone – left behind.

Using case examples in his book *The Brain That Changes Itself*, Dr Norman Doidge asserts, "The discovery of neuroplasticity, that our thoughts can change the structure and function of our brains, even into old age, is the most important breakthrough in our understanding of the brain in four hundred years." A faculty member in the University of Toronto's Department of Psychiatry and Columbia University's Center for Psychoanalytic Training and Research, Doidge believes that our brains can literally change our minds, again and again.[8]

The good news for change practitioners is that our brains are actually free of the effects of lock in and networking, if we want to change – after firstly seeing the need or benefit in making the effort.

Until recently it was thought that our learning was a matter of intelligence, and that regardless of how hard we tried, differences in achievement were due to "ability" or "effort". This belief concentrates almost exclusively on conscious reasoning. According to research undertaken by Professor Guy Claxton of the University of Bristol and detailed in his book "Wise Up, The Challenge of Life Long Learning", good learners need to know when to mull and drift. Learning capability is not fixed at birth and can be expanded as we mature.[9]

Tufts University developmental psychologist Maryanne Wolfe demonstrates that different parts of the brain are used for different types of reading and understanding. This she says has led to parts of the brain trained into the rapid deciphering of text.[10]

For example, readers of English rely more on the parts of the brain that recognise visual shapes, than do readers of Italian. (It is thought that perhaps this stems from the fact that most Italian words 'sound' exactly the way they 'look', while in English many words are pronounced differently to their literal spelling.)

The Net Generation has developed brains that "think" differently, because they didn't have (the same) lock in. When the cost of storage and bandwidth dropped, one-way linear media became two-way. Our brains are able to react interactively, across an immensely vast, new spectrum. Digital guru, virtual reality pioneer, and Silicone Valley veteran Jaron Lanier sees that it's now impossible to work in information technology without also engaging in social engineering. Linked with University of California Berkeley and early development of Microsoft, he reminds us that software development is also the outcome of exceptionally rigid 'lock in'. He sees that, since human endeavours are increasingly driven by the kind of software he's helped to develop, the sum total is that the human mind is more subject to lock in than ever before. While Lanier laments what this means for humankind, he nonetheless agrees that we are changing as people.[11]

So we can see the change, we can see the reason to recognise this change, and we can see that – if we want to – we can also change to meet the challenge. So there can be little reason to resist.

Just like the classic definition of an economic depression, we often don't want to recognise change has happened, until it's past. It's always much easier to cope with change as history.

Social v Organisational

We are increasingly socialising in a way that fits within the boundaries of existing networked intelligence. Our social circles may be widening, but only within the structure that 'fits the mould' of the software we are using. Our expectations are increasingly bounded by our "locked in" social environment.

What this means for Organisational Change is clear; instantly networked intelligence has replaced time-consuming communication, while authority is being replaced by a democracy.

It's not just attitudes that have changed. Insomuch as previously-unused parts of our brain are now being used as never before, there is rewiring underway.

At the heart of any organisation progress is motivation, built around the questions "Why are people involving themselves in this organisational structure, and what do they hope to achieve through it?" While we know linear thinking encouraged depth of thinking, digitally networked thinking encourages breadth of thinking – that is, we used to know a lot about a few things, but now we can know (or find out) fewer things about much more.

As Doctor Samuel Johnston was once quoted by Boswell, "Knowledge is of two kinds. We know a subject ourselves, or we can find information upon it."[12] But, as he may have been quick to add, simply knowing where to find it does not mean we know it. Today, with such information literally at our fingertips, knowing where to find a fact can satisfy our thirst for Johnston's second kind of knowledge, while we believe that we have mastered the first. Otherwise, why would we spend so much time simply 'surfing' knowledge, rather than 'knowing' it to some depth? Much of what we learned before and 'knew' may no be longer valid in this networked thinking world.

What caused social awareness and organisational motivation in a linear, analogue world is unlikely to work well in a digitally networked world. Like an old VHS, it used to work, but is not up to it any more.

Having worked globally with clients as a change agent in the media over 30 years, it's obvious why some economies are expanding, while others stagnate, or go backwards. Early digital adopters, India, China, Korea and Japan, are just ahead of the digital wave.

The Digital Mind

We - and our societies - are changing, as technology is changing us. It frees us to act and think with less cumbersome baggage, to a depth and a rate never known. The job for change practitioners becomes harder.

What may have once been process driven, with step-by-steps, relying on an accepted hierarchy of human interaction must now adapt to quicker, much flatter, organisational information and command structures. One that operates with links and movement, not necessarily the leaders' choice, but the choice of those identified by the individual, in real time.

Our intelligence is networked and filtered by the rigid process of software lock in, which means that no matter how clever an algorithm is, it is, by its very process locked into a finite list of defined instructions.

While our choices are wider and our learning opportunities more profound, there is a growing conformity in the process. We have the chance to search deeper into our preconceived thoughts and ideas, if we are secure in them. We also have the chance to search wider if we are insecure, or feel the need to be more open-minded.

Boards Risk It All

How IT Transformation Projects Create Board Failure

Joanne Flinn and Alexander Budzier

> *"It's not writing–off $200 million, that's rough. It's not the 2 years it took to do the project. It's the impact on the business. It takes 6 months to recover from a major change, 6 months to work out where the project really went wrong, a year to select a new vendor, then 2 years to implement again. That's 5 years lost in the market. This is what's nuclear."*

> *Thomas, CEO of a bank, stood ashen faced as he remembered the recovery, the hours worked, the family time missed, the people fired and jobs lost, the customers let down, and the sheer effort it took to regain lost ground against competitors. Thomas continued "The struggle to keep the company alive cost me my relationship with my family."*

Boards deal with risk and most dedicate a subcommittee to it. While "project investment" is frequently discussed, its evil twin "project risk" is less so. This is a challenge for Boards, who have increasing accountability for business failures. Little support or explicit advice is available for Boards in project risk profiles, particularly the unusual risk profile rising from technology enabled transformation. This chapter helps Boards more effectively deal with project risk at the corporate level.

When one in six large technology based projects (for example Enterprise Resource Planning ERP, cloud or any technology based business transformation) puts a company at risk according to Harvard Business Review in 2011, what can Boards do to reduce this apparently operational risk?

Joanne (Reflective Practitioner) and Alex (Practical Academic) identify two trends that lead to increasing Board accountability for these risks, identify how the concept of wickedness can reduce these risks to Boards and provide practical actions for Boards to take to reduce these risks ~ without moving into operational turf.

Project risk – on the Board agenda

> *"Projects, project risks, it all seems rather operational. That's what our business leaders are there for."*

There is a well-established divide between what is Board and what is Business.[1] However, two trends are driving the shift to certain types of projects being Board Business. The increased investment in and the unusual risk profile of technology projects puts certain projects into risks profiles that fit Board level responsibility. Secondly, legislative norms are increasing Board responsibility. Without a means of profiling 'if and when' a risk is material, Boards will be exposed. We outline these risks and provide a framework to address risks at this governance level.

As they'd say in Asia, if it is going to rain in August, it is better to prepare[*]. This article helps Boards prepare.

Occam's Razor: Keeping things simple

Alexander and Joanne met in 2011, in an Oxford café. He'd just published an article in *Harvard Business Review* about large IT projects putting companies at risk and was well into a PhD focusing on executive decision making and project failure. She was a businesswoman who had just published a book about the corporate cost of project failure.

Over lattés, they asked, "Why do smart executives keep funding projects that cost 200-400% more than expected, deliver 50% less than expected and take two times longer than expected?" With 20 years of data about thousands of projects, they concluded the problem is not a lack of information. Given that many senior executives see large projects fail, the problem clearly isn't lack of personal experience either. While the problem appears simple, it isn't simplistic.

They asked, "Is there any guidance for those who approve the big project spending, like Boards? Is there anything that helps them frame the risks as well as the returns of the investment?" There was none. Boards face an additional challenge: what can they look at or do when theirs is a hands-off role?

---

[*]	Preparation is multi-dimensional. The Chinese character, risk, contains opportunity. Even a humble rice farmer, Chairman of the Board of his small business, makes sure the roof of his house is strong and that the house can stand winds that may come with the rains. He makes sure that water flow systems and storage systems are well suited for his next crop of rice and has seedlings ready to plant, as the rains feed rice.

Showing up ourselves for a moment

Joanne Flinn (based in Singapore, lived in 13 countries):

As a practitioner of change, I've been a Board member, sat on governance committees, and functioned as a project manager, change manager, and project mentor. I've worked with PricewaterhouseCoopers, IBM, NOL-APL, Citibank, Bank Julius Baer, and Olympus. Some projects were business turnarounds, others major technology implementations.

Data showed gaps in assessments, approval, and governance processes as more costly and systemic than I'd realised when I began my research at HEC and the University of Oxford. This lack of data fuelled my subsequent focus on what helps projects succeed (or fail).

Learning both through several decades of experience working in Asia, and the research process at HEC and Oxford, data and models helped refine my practice. The logic and power of the data available today says project management and change management are not enough for results. The use of heavy control-based systems likewise does not create results, but those who use management methods based on what the academics call complex adaptive systems did better.

Terms like presence, wickedness, and emergence entered my vocabulary. My focus shifted from technical systems (technology, process, organisation) into human systems and how these impact value creation. The patterns behind human systems allowed development of predictive algorithms that improve project value creation (ones that identify risk profiles to value creation). Creating simplicity in a complex, multi-dimensional, dynamic, cross-dependent world has become a personal journey.

Alexander Budzier (based in Oxford, lived in 5 countries):

I entered academia to address a burning issue: why do smart people make poor decisions in the project context? My practice began at McKinsey's. It brought me in front of Boards presenting turn-around plans, cost-benefit-analysis, and project capability benchmarks. But often I wondered whether we did more harm than good. Not that these plans and cost-benefit analyses were amiss, quite the opposite: a lot of effort and resources went into them. However, I saw many good plans undone simply by the false belief that everything will go according to plan.

I got interested in why an organisation's decision-makers deal with risk so dysfunctionally. Why do they acknowledge some risks but ignore others? Why do they learn from some failures but not from others? Why do they build risk registers but then wished they were empty? Why are they happy solving issues and managing crises but fail to be proactive?

One of my early mentors told me: "Always make sure that there is space to reflect on what you are doing. If that space is gone you are about to hit an iceberg."

My research at the University of Oxford showed me that this simple advice applies to Boards. The technical term for this particular reflective space is the Outside View, and the rich body of work I reviewed and our own research confirms it: when decision-makers are trapped in the Inside View, risks are ignored and underestimated, the false belief that everything goes according to plan rules, and no learning takes place.

Our experience is that some Boards receive progress reports, milestone reports, metrics, or other potential early warning signs about projects they have approved. It is not always out of sight, nor out of mind. However, we found the frequency and impact of project risk sufficiently high combined with awareness being sufficiently low, that our inquiries shifted from 'there is a problem', to 'why do smart people do this', to 'what can Boards do to succeed?

Reflection on Risk

This chapter provides a reflective space. We begin with data, which is 'a project killer' according to one Board advisor. Our unabashed view is that Boards are smart folks who would prefer to deal with reality rather than hide. We tie these risks to recent legislative shifts that place project risk clearly under the control and responsibility of Boards.

Then we look at the problem of project risk appreciation and leadership to understand what sort of problem it really is. Yes, it is a wicked problem, creating particular challenges in practice for both Boards and the C-Suite. Wicked problems (problems that don't seem to be resolved easily despite good effort and smart people) require wicked management. Finally, we cover key ideas about wicked management and what it can to do to ensure success.

Boards and Project Risk

Data: Profile of an Under-Appreciated Board Risk

Major projects and business transformations are large undertakings. Organisations invest huge effort and many resources into transformations to gain a competitive advantage.[2] Heroes are made through their success, yet equally true, companies and careers can be killed.[3]

While some leaders may act as if stories like Thomas's rarely occur and that the costs of failure are insignificant, recent research challenges this presumption. While data for pure change projects is sparse, evidence for technology-driven change shows that:

- Projects (that is, a deliberate investment in change) cost on average 27.5 percent more than expected[4]
- One in six large projects (IT based transformation) costs two to four times more than expected[5]
- Programmes and portfolios of projects deliver a negative yield[6] of -27.5 to -70 percent.[7]

The data challenges the view that projects *readily* create value. Big projects in the public sphere failing to deliver and over-running their budget are well publicised. While less transparent, data shows the persistence of big project issues[8] in the business world.

The Board of a small UK multinational corporation operating in 14 countries with a $60 million turnover and $4 million profit approved a project to transform operations. This required changes to processes, roles, and technology. The technology component was approved for $2 million over 2 years. Project costs grew to $4 million over 4 years, challenging cash flow and reducing business capacity to respond to other opportunities during that 4 year period.

A globally recognised household name, a manufacturer of family care products was unable to ship product for over a month in South Africa after an ERP implementation.

A major clothing manufacturer operating in over 110 countries introduced new common processes and systems. An initial budget of $5 million grew over 5 years to become a $192.5 charge against earnings. The USA distribution centre was unable to fill orders for a week.

Antiquated business systems needed replacement at a major Asian bank. The Board approved a $200 million dollar programme. Four years later, the bank wrote off $400 million retrenching teams and leadership. Internal estimates suggest that another $400 million of internal effort was also spent. Eight years on, new systems begin to operate providing the new business platform.

Big projects are dangerous to companies when they go wrong. They consume free cash flow, starving other projects and the business of funds, they can damage company reputation and give competitors the opportunity to gain market share.

For Boards, most big projects are an "investment approval process" with governance systems based on size of spend, with the implicit assumption that this aligns with risk exposure. However, spend is not the key determinant of risk profile. Likewise, even after being given the green light, big projects continue to be a risk and governance issue at Board level (highlighted by the earlier statistic about 1 in 6 projects costing 200-400% more than expected).[9] There are discernible risk factors contributing to this variation, it is not simply the size of the project budget.[10]

Milestones and other standard reporting provide hindsight assessment of 'yes, it went off the rails'. For large technology-based projects this comes too late. The juggernaut is in trouble. Boards (and C Suite) need their equivalent of an early warning signal to see risks before they become reality.

This issue is not limited to larger projects, as portfolios of projects can also sum up to a risk[11] relevant at the corporate level.

Another Layer of Risk: Portfolios of Projects

Complex linkages between projects in a portfolio affect the efficiency of said portfolio. Contrary to economic wisdom, project portfolio management is not a zero sum game. Projects are sticky. Divestment is difficult and cross-dependent. Once started, projects are rarely stopped quickly - on average only 3 big projects are abandoned over a 5-year timespan.[12]

Portfolios of projects (operational, IT, risk, internal change) frequently have negative yields. Benchmarks range from -27.5% to -70%, that is, for every dollar spent, only 30 cents returns.

Depending on the relative size of the project portfolio to company Free Cash Flow (FCF), Boards may also find risks arise from either an unexpected value shortfall or an increased demand for additional funds. This reduces operational surplus or eats into company reserves. For listed companies or those with active shareholders, an ability to proactively identify, predict, and manage these risks may become part of expected good Board governance (see next section: Law).

Project and portfolio risks are not linear. We can illustrate this using benchmark data for a $5,000,000 portfolio. These risks may consume substantial additional resources.

Table 1 Illustration of Portfolio Risk - Simple variant risk assessment using portfolio size.

Project Portfolio (size)	$ 5,000,000 (original budget)
Risk Profile (illustrative)	**Additional Spend**
Conservative Variation	$1,375,000
More Probable Variation	$1,650,000
Potential Variation	$3,500,000
Black Swan or Rare Events (1 in 6)	$10,000,000

Source: Sauer, Flinn, Flyvbjeg, and Budzier.

This variation suggests there is a long term systemic performance problem that has not been eradicated by the increasing use of project management and change management. The data shows that risks are not increasing in a straight line – they escalate. Fortunately multifactor risk assessments calibrated by predictive algorithms can identify specific project risk to:

- Incremental budget
- Value creation
- Risk to strategy
- Corporate sustainability

Project (and portfolio) underperformance has been a systemic risk with limited signs of improvement over the last 20 years. This begs the question: Why care now?

Increasing IT dependency in business and thus projects leads to higher risks in project portfolios. More agile developments and smaller projects have increased risk visibility and increased complexity of dependencies in project portfolios.

The issue could be seen simply as a matter of corporate spend and internal good governance with a worst-case risk to firm survival. However the high monetary risk of technology projects increases as project size and complexity increases, and this trend will continue.

That technology is influencing our business and lives is clear – social trends, digital thinking, and use of personal data (and thus new uses of technology and business risk from the application of technology).

The cost, scale and use of technology in the twenty-first century are not the only trend driving a stronger Board role in governance. A legislative trend likewise points to increasing Board accountability for projects.

Law: Legislation Pressure Increases Board Accountability for Project Risk and Failure

Shareholders, investors, and customers expect more of Boards. The trend for increased Board accountability for risk, including project risk, is clear across the globe, moving past commentary and recommendations into legislation as seen in Table 2.

For Boards, project risks to an organisation are both substantial and predictable. The legal trend is also clear. Yet, Boards have a specific remit – it is not to manage but to govern, by assessing risks, and ensuring controls are adequate.

Table 2 Legislation and Standards Upholding a Board Role

Country	Legislation & Standards	Relevance
UK (Ireland has similar legislation)	UK Corporate Governance Code (2012)	"The Board's role is to provide entrepreneurial leadership of the company within a framework of prudent and effective controls which enables risk to be assessed and managed." (p. 11). The Board is responsible for determining the nature and extent of the significant risks it is willing to take in achieving its strategic objectives (p. 21)
USA	Sarbanes-Oxley (SOX)	Annual certification of internal controls is required.
Australia	AS 8015—2005 Standards Australia	ISO 38500 announcement targeted to the Boards of Directors guides how they judge the IT organisation while Val IT represents guidance to the CIO organisation about the processes they put in place to demonstrate their performance to the Boards of Directors (IBM[13])
International Standards	ISO/IEC 38500:2008, *Corporate governance of information technology*	This standard is targeted at the Board of an organisation, to assist the Board in delivering the maximum value from IT and information assets across the organisation (IT Governance[14])
South Africa	King III Report on Governance 2009	Emphasis is placed on… <ul><li>*Risk based internal audit* - This will enable companies to place more reliance upon internal controls, which internal audit will verify/assure.</li><li>*IT Governance* - IT governance is important as it is a major operational risk. (p. 4)</li></ul>

Board Reality

Boards may not be experts in projects, in technology, or in change management. While organisations typically employ experts for each of these professional knowledge sets, they are rarely found on Boards.

Boards may struggle with a generational divide. Many Board members are from a generation in which technology is something someone else does, and projects are used to implement strategy, some distance away from Board oversight.

It's not that Boards don't expect to see large spend. It's that the risk profile of technology-based projects is different to spend on a new manufacturing plant. It's easy to overlook a risk that seems either 'someone else's problem' (operational) or out of (generational) comfort zone.

Regulatory standards increase governance expectations. Norms are shifting and they are shifting fast. This opens up the potential for legal action for breach of fiduciary duty through inadequate project governance at the Board level.

These standards provide little guidance to Boards about project governance.[15] Yet the magnitude of risk requires Boards to gain insight into projects, portfolios, and their results.

To be direct, there is a very human side to acknowledging data and recognising risks.

The World is Neither Simple nor Solvable – it's Wicked

Defining project objectives, securing funding, and obtaining all the right resources are intensely political processes, likely to bias data to look 'good.'[16] Multiple external service providers need to be screened and selected. Each of these steps requires complex, often political, trade-offs with other parts of the organisation.

Most organisations select projects based on profitability via Net Present Value (NPV), payback periods, internal rates of return, or benefit-cost ratio. On one hand, project selection is easier because projects are linked to shareholder value. On the other hand, this process creates perverse incentives. Project appraisals become no more than well-dressed marketing material competing for funds, and rarely is there a soundly assessed risk profile.[17] This incentivises the party seeking the funds to downplay risks.[18] A Board may make an investment decision based on optimistic funding and independent of risk.

Yet risk is an important element of the governance decision. Simple problems have straight forward, linear, causal relationships and can be solved by analytical methods.[19] Governance of big projects is rarely simple or linear.

Big projects cannot simply shrink to a better size. Big projects are a response to a complex, interacting set of problems. Big projects involve multiple parties. Big projects pursue multi-layered solutions in a changing environment. Big projects are wicked.

Wicked Reality

Wickedness in this case is not a moral judgment but a description of a particular type of situation (or problem).[20] A project is wicked when it fits the following criteria:

1. The problem and solution are intertwined.

    Practical example:

    Replacing a core business system or responding to a regulatory change; requires technology, data, processes, people, behaviours, policies, etc. to change. The solution has many parts. Each part has its trade-offs, which in turn pose new problems and re-define old problems.

    The problem may not be fully understood at project start. With progress towards solutions, understanding of the project changes.

2. It is not clear if and when the project is successful.

    Practical example:

    Every stakeholder has their own, often conflicting, idea of what constitutes success. Additionally, it's hard to tell when the project is done. Is it done when it is implemented? Is it done when results are achieved? Particularly in IT projects, 'good enough' is declared when some closure is reached or when resources are depleted, stakeholders lose interest, or political realities have moved on. In technical terms: 'the problem lacks a stopping rule.'

3. The choice is between good and bad, not true or false; the criteria for 'good enough' are a negotiated judgment.

    Practical example:

Defining project success as "We spent $5 million dollars in 12 months" can be assessed with a true or false but would hardly be considered a success. In practice, it's more likely to be, "We will spend $5 million and we want x, y, z (so do your best)." Implicit is that this is the total spend – yet in reality, projects that don't deliver create negative effects in the organisation, including additional work for other projects, work-arounds in the business (adding to operational cost and risk), and disillusionment.

4. The consequences (often unintended) are not clear.

   Practical example:

   Early decisions in an IT project lock in the organisation. Implementing system x has consequences for operations, maintenance, and interplay with other systems, among others. However, these early decisions are often made before all relevant stakeholders have been activated and involved.

   In technical terms, "The circle of action is larger than the circle of foresight." This entails positive and negative unintended consequences.

5. The problem appears to be unique.

   Practical example:

   A problem like 'how to grow revenue in our business' is affected by the situation of business context, strategy, partners, competitors, and the economy. surrounding the specific business, which in turn makes everybody believe that they solve a unique problem... but growing revenue is really a common problem.

6. Different stakeholders have different, often contradictory, perspectives on the solution.

   Practical example:

   Market share is a result of economic activity, customer service expectations, services delivered, production quality, and competitor activity. Which ones are in play now? Which will come into play as the project progresses?

   The sales director needs a new CRM system. His department buys a web-based CRM. They start using it and then require IT to integrate into the enterprise customer database that feeds into finance, controlling, back office, customer service operations, and more. Each of those holds very different ideas about the ideal solution.

Information systems projects are frequently considered to be unique and complex, but not wicked. They are seen as an engineering challenge; however, practical experience is re-enforced by research - organisational and social aspects have more significant effects on performance and outcomes.[21] Technology projects are foremost human systems. Human systems are frequently wicked.

Many project and project portfolios are unacknowledged as wicked. As a result, project forecasts, governance, project methodologies, and project outcomes are inappropriately formulated for their context.[22] Track records of success are rarely considered. They also take time to build.

Organisations and executives hide their wickedness. It is common to simply break a big, complex, wicked project into smaller pieces.[23] While this relieves the project manager, the value and risk for the organisation has shifted into the portfolio. The portfolio of these projects is still complex and wicked.[24] Most organisations are ill equipped to appropriately manage their (IT) project portfolio and its wicked risks.[25] If you govern a major project investment or portfolio of investments, understand and see its wickedness. Ask:

1. Which solution has been chosen? By whom? What problem(s) is really addressed?
2. What are the success criteria? Where is the finish line? What is 'good and bad'?
3. Who makes key decisions, like project sign-off? Who else should?
4. Which key trade-offs are required? Which other projects are required to truly deliver value? How will unintended consequences be identified?
5. What makes the project complex and unique? Where are the risks to value?
6. What are the goals to be achieved in the next quarter? What is the political reality of this project?

A practical test for the presence of wicked problems and projects is as follows:

- Many parts interact: This is true of most strategies, large projects, programmes, and project portfolios.
- Different values are in play: This is true if multiple stakeholders are involved or affected by the project.

For example: an IT infrastructure project may be complex but if it does not require job losses, it is less likely to be wicked. In contrast, a new strategy, an ERP system, or a culture change project, may be both complex and wicked because human behavioural change is required.

Wickedness Creates Challenges

In the Boardroom, wicked problems lead to unlearning four key operating assumptions:

- Full Rationality: Information is available
- Certainty: Knowledge of what will happen
- Full insight: We are experienced (not ignorant)
- Simplicity: Linear cause and effect

When dealing with wicked projects, more effective operating assumptions are as follows:

From Full Rationality to Practical Rationality with Heuristics[26]

While we might desire definitively rational and perfect knowledge, we have learned otherwise. In a wicked world, knowing is limited since perfect information is not possible. Forecasting methods and theories of economic reality are also limited when dealing with rare or black swan events.[27] The standard go-to solution of "we need more science in this!" does not work. In this space, we operate beyond the limits of the theory of economic rationality.[28]

In this world, learned heuristics are more accurate than many statistical methods.[29] Art is more important than science. Heuristics are practical rules of thumb. They are shortcuts to making decisions. Often they fail, but often they are right, and they are fast: this is practical rationality.

> "Double it (the estimate) and hope for the best."
> Board Member of a VC describing their approach
> to risk assessment

Heuristics are heavily used by medics, applied scientists and fire fighters. [30]

From Certainty to Probability

Predictability is limited.[31] Data is hardly available for comparable identical situations. When processing data, logical fallacies distort our thinking: cognitive biases, misplaced causality, and politics. When we cite statistics that show 'project killer' statistics like: '1 in 6 projects cost at least 2-4 times what is expected' or 'Portfolio of projects conservatively under deliver by a third', we get a typical reaction to this uncomfortable knowledge, including: "we are better than this;" "it is not applicable to us;" "this was a unique issue that will not happen again;" or "this is a project killer (we don't want to know)."[32]

These responses don't stack up to the facts.

> *"Why would we check the risk of a project, we've decided to do it." - A Board Member of a NYSE listed company*

Why, indeed? Confidence is a required executive trait. Decision-making power resides with people, not spread sheets. Data is a reality check. Optimism bias (and politics) exists at the Board level as much as it does at operational levels. Logical biases do not go away simply by acknowledging their existence.[33] We need to unlearn certainty and re-learn probability. Conventional assessment processes like statistical forecasting, Delphi studies, scenario, and expert judgment don't anticipate rare events. One in six is considered rare, yet in reality **17 percent** of projects in your portfolio blow up.

Convert lack of certainty into predictability through the power of probability.

From Full Insight to Muddy Governance

Most Boards maintain a hands-off approach to business operations. This hands-off mindset is appropriate for simple projects, but large projects threaten firm survival and the systemic risks expose Boards to breaches of duty.

As a practitioner, wickedness requires unlearning the desire for full insight and accepting muddy governance. Full insight is not possible, but neither is not doing anything. Not making appropriate enquiries could considered negligence.

Muddy governance

At the board level muddy governance consists of simple indicators and knowing when to get muddy (such as stepping into a Steering Committee or Portfolio Management Committee) through assessing risks of failure, risks to value creation, and risks to project delivery reduce risk.

Many of these risks are predictable. However admitting to risks may be politically dangerous. Boards may need neutral, independent means of gaining insight into these risks and the opportunities that come with successfully dealing. (Heuristics supporting and when to step in can be found in the next section, Wicked Risk Management for Boards.)

Reducing portfolio wastage and project write-offs[34] has direct bottom line value and often has staff performance benefits as well, since most people enjoy working on projects that succeed.

From Simplicity to Adaptive Complexity

Within wickedness is complexity. Unlearn the traditional management logic of breaking up complexity until it becomes simple. Reductionism is inadequate and inappropriate. Appreciating the interaction between different parts of the business better reflects reality of system complexity.

Systems thinking sciences show that emergence is normal in complex systems (new properties appear that are different to the sum of the parts) and can be the reason why organisations exist. The tight coupling between parts of projects and in portfolios means that input changes create unexpected outcomes.

Explicitness about where accountability resides within the system helps (such as operations, management, strategy, leadership, governance, and culture). Accountability has multiple parts – see a data set, escalated to the appropriate level, and get the appropriate group to take a decision. Some problems are visible in one level but must be dealt with on a higher level. This leads to unlearning responsibility for project success based on a single project. Instead of control spans, in reality, Boards need to govern networks of responsibility.

Not only are wicked organisations a complex system of technological and social elements, they are adaptive. Both technology and social components constantly change. Pressing for stability and simplicity prevents change. Bigger pressure and longer inertia generate a bigger blow-up. When Boards under-acknowledge the complex adaptive reality, they create hidden risks and imposes hidden costs on the future organisation.

While the wait-and-see approach to the implications of being both complex and adaptive is appealing, the cumulative cost evidenced earlier, and illustrated by Thomas's story, underlines the need for early indicators of danger, observation, and preventive action (risk mitigation).[35]

The black and white world of rationality, certainty, knowledge, and reductionism is in fact a far more dynamic, uncertain, complex world with many shades of grey and much more colour, and, fortunately, one that has its own simplicities.

Wicked Risk Management for Boards

Unlearning textbook ideas that don't stack up in reality, learning the simplicity of heuristics, muddy governance, probability, and complex adaptability are not the only objectives. Boards have an additional challenge. Most meet infrequently and operate via subcommittees.

Each Board meeting has a full agenda – decisions can be easily deferred to another meeting or down the organisational food chain. With projects, delays to decision making only increase risk and cost. The multiplicity of factors in wicked risks means diffused accountability will frequently get lost. The Board is truly where the buck should stop, as roads lead to the centre.

Acknowledging this, we turn to action. The actions that Boards can take based on heuristics, probabilistic thinking, adaptive complexity, and muddy governance regarding timing of the following:

- Mentor – reduce risks through guidance
- Monitor – reduce risks through reporting and controls
- Meddle – reduce risk by getting muddy

Mentor: Assign Systemic Issues to Respective Board Committees

A single project performing poorly may be easily dismissed as an issue of local management. Systemic patterns of poor performance are often signals that point to systemic issues.[36] Some issues are amenable to Board intervention; others can be influenced via Board policy and scrutiny. Boards can take on a mentoring perspective of encouraging project performance.

For example:

- **Finance Sub-Committee:** Finance practices affect the way business cases are put together, what is included or excluded, and thus add rigor to project budgets. Finance Sub-Committee can adjust investment escalation criteria to include risk profile factors and ask Audit to review completeness of project budgets.
- **HR Sub-Committee:** Leadership and HR practices that affect human behaviour can impact adaptability and acceptance of change. The HR Sub-Committee can look into policies that bias the organisation from adapting to

change or to escalating risk in the interest of other KPIs and performance rewards.

- **Risk Sub-Committee:** Operational risks from poor project implementation can be substantive. Sustainability risks from project variations are also significant. Risk Sub-Committee can adjust the risks it expects to have reported and set expectations for better reporting of early warning signs.
- **Main Board:** Business leadership and IT policies affect the way technology-based change is introduced. This is where it begins and ends. Many projects have technology components, many strategies are implicitly based on successful delivery of technology. It is the 21st Century.

Monitor: Establish Trigger Thresholds for Project Free Cash Flow Consumption

The high monetary risk profile and the Board business risk create a challenge for risk analysis. The distance from the Board to the facts of the situation limits certain forms of insight. Heuristics are a practical solution. Two heuristics provide useful decision making insight.

- Exception Ratios: Project spend to Free Cash Flow
- Visual Cues

The ratio of project and portfolio spend to free cash flow consumption is a practical heuristic used by Boards to prioritise threatening risks. The heuristic may be adapted to local circumstances, e.g., different thresholds, yields, and probability.[37] The heuristic works, if used at least quarterly.[38]

Table 3. Heuristic: Project and Portfolio Spend to Free Cash Flow

Free Cash Flow Threshold	Boards can monitor	Purpose of Board review
2%	Projects with this budget or spend	Approval & Visibility
3%[1]	Capital-at-Risk from either a single project or a portfolio. Expect tracking of risk patterns so that business leadership can identify systemic patterns. It is preferable for a track record of project performance and risk to be established early on prior to capital being at risk. As a Board, you may need this data when it gets muddy.	Get Muddy – review risk patterns, assign actions and monitor results – this is a wicked project in action.
5%	Projects with this budget or spend plus their current results risk register	Monitoring
10%	Project Portfolios (single or collective) and their expected yield. Expected Yield measures expected results, inputs (investment) and the probability of success.	Monitoring & Control

---

[1] In banking, a non-performing loan ratio on a portfolio of loans of -3% is considered a governance issue. -10% is business critical, it requires the remaining 90% of the portfolio to make up for lost capital as well as contribute to the required level of return.

A second heuristic for monitoring is visual. Some Board members process tables of figures better, others visually rich reporting. Using both aids issues identification and decision making.[39]

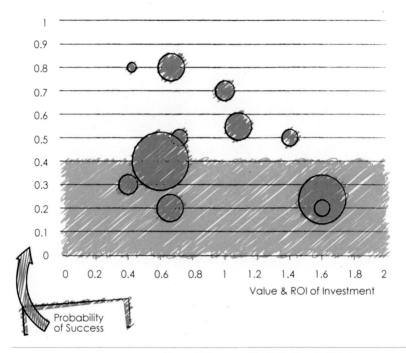

Figure 1: Program/Portfolio Results Risk Assessment

For example: a portfolio of projects or a programme and its subprojects can be reported crisply on a single report showing value in investment (the size of the circle) and the value/risk profile. High risk projects are in the orange zone.[40] Boards may also see relationship between projects (the links) and time series data.

Muddy: Stepping into Action

The first two actions, Mentoring and Monitoring, apply Drucker's dictum "What gets measured, gets done." Measuring risk reduces the risk of negligence as a relevant reporting process demonstrates care. It is harder to say "You ignored a risk and lack adequate control processes" with mentoring and monitoring processes. These heuristics add tremendous value to the business due to early risk avoidance. Every million dollars of free cash flow saved is a million dollars that can be put to other good use.

There are also times where Boards may need to take further action.

Risk spotting

Black Swans are easy to find when one knows where to look. There are services that can assess projects for Black Swan risk based on validated benchmarks and predictive algorithms. Boards provide oversight to ensure this occurs and that action is taken to create the desired result.

In a wicked, complex, adaptive world, course corrections are natural and necessary. Publicly recognising the need for a course correction runs counter to many business practices and corporate culture (to admit to this might be seen as admitting to a mistake and career suicide). Boards may need to take proactive action in the form of specific change programmes with their senior leadership team.

Risk prevention

Thomas used the term "nuclear" when referring to the impact of project failure. Preventive medicine requires good habits and periodically checks good health. The Mentoring and Monitoring heuristics highlight when Boards may need to call for a healthcheck. That's getting muddy!

Boards need to get muddy to pinpoint and impact systemic issues. Most other levels of the organisation lack the political will to identify and change these issues. How may roles really focus on long-term sustainability of business over of the next quarterly results? If not the Board, who will ask which systemic practices corrode the free cash flow? These are big picture issues.

Ultimate accountability sits with the Board but the source of these issues lies in all levels of the organisation with responsibility shared across a wide network. Boards need to investigate with multiple lenses as to what bad habits threaten firm health and what to do about them. These diagnoses and remedies themselves are a wicked problem.

Risk responsibility network

The distribution of risk visibility and risk accountability through different levels of the business from Board to operations creates new links between project teams doing most of the project work, the business of who deals with the results of the project (and pays the bills), and the Board who is ultimately responsible for major risks and performance in the eyes of shareholders and the law.

In a wicked muddy world, new communications, escalation practices, audit roles, and expectations emerge. This is a complex adaptive change programme itself. Junior or mid-management staff may be able to see a risk that only the Board or C Suite can deal with.

In the UK, the executive have been held responsible for operational failures on the basis that cost cutting pressures had generated the culture that lead to the failures. The Monetary Authority of Singapore fined one bank $200 million for problems that apparently arose in an outsourced data centre. The risk responsibility network extends outside of the business.

At a practical level, Boards can get started by informally reviewing projects, by engaging more independent reviews of projects that consider risks from the Board perspective, and establish discussion forums between themselves and the team. Local cultural norms, political responses, and reactions also need to be managed in the process.

Get Muddy or Pay Up and Insure

Increasing use of technology exposes businesses and Boards to new risk profiles. Legislative changes are increasing Board accountability for these risks. Wickedness provides a framework for understanding the deeper challenge. Wickedness is only worrisome when it is unexpected, unacknowledged, or denied.

These days, wicked projects can and do "live long and prosper", as can the Boards and businesses that need them. Unlearn faulty solutions and replace them with wicked risk management for Boards: mentor, monitor, and get muddy.

Deviance, Discovery, and Delight

Two Journeys into Positive Deviance

Jane Lewis and Roberto Saco

One theme, two intertwined perspectives: in the foreground, a change practitioner's personal journey to insight, enlightenment, and making a real difference; in the background, positive deviance itself makes the long journey from the developing to the developed world.

By Way of Introduction

"It was the best of times, it was the worst of times, it was the age of wisdom, it was the age of foolishness ..." and so, with apologies to Dickens, and the Tale of Two Cities, begins our story. It is a story of two journeys: one personal, the other contextual.

Learning from Positive Deviance (PD) originator Jerry Sternin's dictum "[You will] only be able to understand it when you have done it," Jane Lewis plunged in, discovering an entirely new way of getting things done with some unusual suspects. Her journey took her to Denmark, Wales, The National College of School Leadership, the Department of Health's top management team, and the HEC/Oxford CCC (Ecole des Hautes Etudes Commerciales/Oxford Consulting and Coaching for Change) programme, as a tutor.[1]

Jane's personal journey with her collaborators and helpers added to the knowledge of implementing positive deviance in the developed world and built on Jerry's legacy, all while making a real difference in lives and communities – teaching people to become self-sufficient and creating "communities of capability."

Jane's story takes place within the larger tale of PD as it migrates from South East Asia and Africa to the shores of the Americas and Europe.

Roberto Saco reflects on this development: how can a method developed in the rice paddies of Asia be successful – in a brilliant example of reverse innovation - in helping eradicate MRSA infections in the West? [MRSA is short for Methicillin-resistant Staphylococcus Aureus, bacteria responsible for several difficult-to-treat and at times mortal infections in humans].

While successful in social applications, the use of PD has had mixed results in the developed world, particularly in for-profit settings. Roberto explores: what obstacles appeared in PD's journey west, and how have these obstacles led to other applications and directions in the US and Europe? Following dissemination patterns not unlike those of many social innovations, PD goes where the network is, finding friendly environments in places and organisations that can fine tune its use to the principles underlying positive change.

PD is embedded in a family of positive approaches for social and behavioural change, and can be an appropriate tool for the current change environment.

Both stories, Jane's experiential and forward journey and Roberto's review of PD's development in the West, tell the tale not of two cities as our opening suggested, but of two ways to describe the same social movement, conveying the deep emotional investment of practitioners and their communities as well as the broad sweep of recent history with a bearing on PD outcomes. These two journeys are intertwined: the individual practitioner is enmeshed in the broader movement, while the movement is driven by individuals.

In the beginning

US relations with Vietnam in the early 1990s were difficult. The Hanoi regime was on the State Department's list of non-desirables, and there were few Americans in the country. A trade embargo alienated the Vietnamese government from any US initiative, private or public.

In the Philippines, Jerry Sternin headed Save the Children (USSC), a US-based NGO providing care and care strategies to children in the developing world.[2] The USSC asked Jerry and his wife Monique to move to Hanoi and implement the programme in Vietnam. Although the effects of the war of liberation and unification were receding into the past, Vietnam was still a very poor country. Between 60 and 70 percent of all Vietnamese children under the age of five were malnourished. Classical developmental remedies had been tried, but provided only short-term relief.

Jerry described the situation:

> The reasons for the failure were not difficult to discern:
>
> a) Villagers were passive programme beneficiaries, who were neither encouraged nor required to change any of the underlying behaviours/practices which led to their children's malnutrition;
>
> b) The nutritional gains which were realised during the programme's implementation were completely based on external food resources which were no longer accessible to villagers after the implementing agency departed; and

> *c) The major focus of the programme was on providing additional food, with little or no attention paid to improving the all-important child caring, and health-seeking behaviours associated with nutritional status. In short, "they came, they fed, they left" and nothing had changed.*[3]

The expert-driven approach to solving malnutrition did not work in Vietnam and the Vietnamese government did not have the resources to solve a problem affecting millions of children. The Sternins were told they had a six-month visa to solve what seemed to be an intractable problem. They had minimal time to search for a solution or develop an approach. Under time pressure and faced with scepticism from the Vietnamese government, Jerry knew he had to find an existing strategy to deal with his challenges. His experiences in the Far East and his knowledge of approaches in the nutrition field led to experimentation that evolved into the positive deviance approach.

In the 1980s, investigators at the Tufts School of Nutrition, led by Dr. Marian Zeitlin, found in study after study that some malnourished children are rehabilitated more quickly than others receiving the same treatment in the same clinical facility. The researchers identified the factors influencing better outcomes and labelled the successful cases "positive deviants." The research was documented and language for the approach developed, but a practical and programmatic methodology did not exist.

The Sternins began work on their own version of positive deviance in the Quang Xuong District in Thanh Hoa province, almost 200 kilometres south of Hanoi. With research of his own, Jerry discovered that in every community there are a number of "positive deviants whose special practices or behaviours enable them to outperform or find a better solution to a problem than his neighbour [or cohort] who has access to the same resources."[4] His course of action was to find the positive deviants who had already incorporated effective strategies to combat malnutrition, study these practices, and perpetuate the practices with the help of the parents as teachers and coaches, and ensuring their sustainability without external resources.

Jerry stresses, however, that the approach is context-dependent. For example, some parents were feeding children more frequently; others used a diet that differed from the norm made up completely of local and/or unusual ingredients. Applied positive deviance was born in the villages of Vietnam in a desperate attempt to better the life of impoverished villagers and their children. Over the years, Vietnamese communities formed a veritable practical university, instituting and amplifying the concept of positive deviance and bringing relief to more than 50,000 children in 250 communities with a combined population of over 2.2 million people.

How Positive Deviance Ignited a Personal Passion

Learning about new approaches to solving what are termed "wicked" problems (unusual, extremely puzzling, and intriguing issues) at the Oxford/HEC CCC programme, Jane was particularly captivated by the Sternins' approach to intractable problems. Their solution seemed a practical way of supporting people to "act their way into a new way of thinking," which could work well with her public sector clients, who had grown sceptical of culture change exercises and wary of management consultants.

Roberto's dissertation topic was positive deviance, while Jane's involved using positive deviance's principles in middle management. They formed a long-term collaboration and friendship, proof of the way in which positive deviance creates communities of interest. As part of the CCC programme, Hala El Farouki invited them along with other alumni as keynote speakers at her home country's gathering. They were fortunate that Jerry and Monique Sternin accepted an invitation too. The presentation by the Sternins inspired Jane's personal journey with positive deviance, and detailed research provided by Roberto aided her further. Jane's mission became bringing positive deviance to the UK and using it to release potential in people that other approaches seemed unable to.

What is Positive Deviance (PD)?

There are at least two ways to answer this question. One answer proceeds down the route of values and principles. The other is addressed by methodology. While the principles of PD have not been universally agreed to - it is not a catechism, and the Sternins shied away from strict uniformity - some working principles apply. We have focused on six:

1. Deviance is everywhere.
2. Deviance is a solution you can find now.
3. Deviance entails ownership (not buy in).
4. Deviance invites community wisdom.
5. Deviance supplies knowledge through practice.
6. Deviance means you adapt and repeat.

There is no positive deviance without positive deviants; fortunately, in most communities, there are people who successfully address the issues and problems, without external or special resources. Sometimes the knowledge is latent; we've all heard the apocryphal story about the factory worker who reveals to a consultant the solution to a decades-old problem. When asked why he hadn't told management, the old man replies "Because no one ever asked me." Positive deviance solicits and honours the views of the outliers, possibly for the first time.

The dictum "You won't understand a problem until you've solved it" is embedded in the second principle of PD. Paralysis by analysis often dooms efforts to solve a problem. PD cuts through the clutter, emphasising finding solutions that exist today, already somewhere in the system.

Jerry was fond of saying: "Don't decide about me without me." The heart of the third principle is that it is not enough to obtain buy-in. Sustainable solutions require ownership, and ownership in turn requires personal discovery. Buy-in is what you do to others to obtain their compliance; ownership is the process that others undertake to arrive at their own solutions.

Positive deviance invites community wisdom. "You have to sit in the marketplace," Jerry said. Data and evidence gathered via observation and analysed by the community reveals patterns of daily life. These patterns become the insights, the "A-has!" of discovery for the community.

The fifth principle reverses the dictum that from knowledge emerges practice. On the contrary, through practice people work their way into a new knowledge. The standard has been in effect for a long time and habits are not discarded easily. Upending the standard requires evidence, consistency, and lots of practice until a new standard comes into being.

The sixth principle involves adaptation and amplification. "'Plug and play' is about computers, not people," we'd heard Jerry say. Each community and each problem is subtly different, even when dealing with the same theme. The process of discovery is essential to dealing with the variation inherent in human problem solving. Discovery empowers and provides acceleration for scalability.

Jerry Sternin was no methodologist: "I don't know what's out there; I only know what I know." Therefore, the PD method is described in many various ways and comprising many different steps. However, most practitioners agree that PD, like innovation, involves at least four stages: Define, Determine, Discover, and Design.

Define

In the first phase, define the community needs. Conduct situational analysis and clearly outline your objectives. Identify in detail the problem to be solved, stating the problem as the standard model. This is the way things are today: x% of the children are malnourished. Conversely, state the optimal condition: This is what we would like to happen: y% of the children is healthy. Appreciative Inquiry and positive therapies are applicable here.

Determine

Identify positive deviants, the people successfully operating outside the standard model. Look for individuals in the community exhibiting the desired outcomes: Are there families in the community who have well-nourished children?

Discover

It is obviously not enough to discover the positive deviants; what matters are the practices that make them deviants. During the third phase, analyse findings from the second phase and assess deviant practices: why are these particular children healthy? What useful and transferable practices can be used by every family in the community?

Design

Finally, design community-based interventions for sustainable change so that others can assess and practice the new behaviours; for example set up a community kitchen so other families observe what successful deviants feed their children, and so observers can practice new recipes.

Many small details lead to a successful PD implementation; these principles guide a practitioner through the variations of such details. The specificity of the situation may require improvisation or iteration, but the principles are consistent from one application to another.

A Movement in the West

Jerry Sternin exemplified the principles of positive deviance - warm, supportive, outward looking, and respectful. He mentored Jane through her initial UK project, but sadly, he passed away before its completion. His positive and uplifting memorial service gave us a chance to meet with key characters in the PD story, including Dr Jon Lloyd, instigator of the US MRSA project; Lars Thuesen, a fellow CCC graduate, who applied PD in the Danish prisons service; and Mark Munger, a trusted PD facilitator for the problem-definition stage of Jane's project.

By 2010, Jane had carried out organisational and community PD projects, lectured on these experiences. Richard Pascale finished a collaborative book with Jerry and Monique Sternin, distilling their experiences and projects in the West, particularly the US MRSA programme, exploring why PD has not been more widely implemented by leaders and change practitioners.[5] The book coincided with the Saïd Business School's interest in Jane's UK work, and her firm co-sponsored a practice research workshop at Egrove Park in May 2010, bringing together the authors, Saïd Fellow Keith Ruddle, Richard Pascale, Monique Sternin, and Jon Lloyd and Randa Wilkinson from the Positive Deviance Initiative. It was a crowded event, enabling connections to create new opportunities for applying PD in organisations broadly.

Key take-aways were:[6]

- PD works best where the efficacy and influence of authority is low, within existing power structures and social networks, and at different levels.
- PD relies on diagnostic and facilitative expertise, not expertise in the problem under review.

- The social proof of the data is critical.
- PD engenders a collaborative culture without culture change as its principal goal.

An open mind and willingness to take personal responsibility are fundamental to the PD ethos, encouraging learning and sharing beyond specific problem-solving exercises.

As PD rolled out in the UK through lectures and projects, it collected a small but growing group of adherents. Supporters formed an advisory group, comprising representatives from the Home Office, senior local authority strategists, and the Audit Commission. Thanks to Keith Ruddle, and Keith Leslie of Deloitte, the message has reached even senior government levels.

First Steps in the UK

The spread of positive deviance was hampered by the lack of training available from first-hand users. Jerry and Monique Sternin provided what mentoring they could, but the Positive Deviance Initiative focused on projects in the developing world, and their new team had little time to offer.

PD is a way of working, more than a distinct end-to-end process. Each case was approached differently in Pascale and Sternins' book *The Power of Positive Deviance*. Existent training materials, while shared openly and willingly, were primarily intended for developing world audiences. The Danish prison programme benefitted from Mark Munger's input but UK authorities could not import consultants from the US in austere times. It was a lonely path to tread as a UK pioneer.

Jane and her team learned much from several projects. The projects were a mix of organisational and community development challenges. The data collection process inherent in PD makes it possible to assess progress from the start. The projects were perceived by their sponsors to have delivered good results. Jane's team is now focusing on post-hoc evaluation for further refinement.

Reclaiming time in Hertfordshire

A regional team of social workers in Hertfordshire had issues with case recording and time management. Through the PD "define" phase, they discovered they were not spending nearly as much time on paperwork as they thought - 25 per cent of their time, not 80 percent. Data collection showed that some staff spent almost 30 percent of their time fielding phone calls from clients' carers and relatives, while others spent substantially less. The "diagonal slice" [7] PD team (made up of administrator, social work student, team leader, occupational therapist and social workers) discovered another team's successful practice of sending letters to carers, acknowledging the clients in the system and telling them what to expect going forward. This team allocated specific administrators to field remaining calls, since supervisors had a better overview of the situation. Other workers discovered ways of hyperlinking documents to reduce input duplication in the computer system, while other shortcuts saved each worker one to two hours a week, and enabled quicker response time to clients needing home adaptations.

Growing capability and quick wins in Gosport

By the time the Gosport projects began, *The Power of Positive Deviance* had been published and provided a crucial roadmap. Jane converted her organisation, Woodward Lewis, into a positive deviance-consulting firm. They tapped a longstanding, trusting business relationship with the local council and were given grant money to train a facilitator cohort, mentoring four community projects.

The first project targeted teen parents. In Gosport, an area in Hampshire with the highest rate of teen pregnancy, Jane and her colleagues trained a manager at a local Surestart children's centre. The manager advertised "tea-time tweets," informal get-togethers for young parents, on Facebook. Although its use did not adhere to official policy, the Facebook page brought together a group of young parents, using a PD discussion style to find and examine the parents' issues. Rather than offering a taught programme, the informal style attracted and retained a large group of local teen parents.

The teens learned from each other, discovering solutions to their stressors for themselves. They all admitted that they wouldn't have listened to adults, and a strong bond formed in the group. This group went on to work with high-risk pupils in their old school, one with a particularly high percentage of the teen pregnancies in the area. While the group was required to follow national curriculum, their approach was consultative and fun. For example, they staged a "Price is Right" competition to show how expensive it was to have a baby and to raise awareness of the isolation and hard work involved. They all were accredited as level 3 teaching assistants and the core group returned to school for further education, most of them graduating with social care qualifications. During the year of the project, the school's conception rate dropped from ten pregnancies per year to three. The council's chief executive reported that three years on, people still talk about this project with admiration and surprise.

The other PD effort focused on the Gosport children's relatively low educational attainment (particularly boys), as measured by the national Early Years Foundation Stage profile. The Children's Centre aimed for parents to recognise their role as first educators, usually presented as a lesson or seminar-type session. Woodward Lewis formed a PD group from parents, to look at early years challenges and find successful practices in the community.

Bureaucratic hurdles added to difficulties (including required criminal background checks, strict curricula needs, and time constraints). The PD group was limited in its ability to consult with other parents and pre-schools in the community. One determined mother, Jez, took the lead and decided to try "speed PD." She was allocated four two-hour slots at the centre, recruited a group of eight other mothers, again through Facebook, and in each session did a reduced version of the four positive deviance stages.

They defined a problem: lack of "messy play" for the children; discovered that each had skills enabling them to provide a messy play experience; designed a play session; and ran it in the final week. The programme retained all eight mums in each session (something almost unheard of), their achievements and confidence were measured through the process. Their feedback was outstanding. It turned out that a vital aspect was that Jez, the lead mother, was "one of them." One year later the group still gathered to support each other.

This group of mothers presented their project to the Gosport Parents Conference, action they would not have thought possible a year earlier. This case was also presented to the National College of School Leadership's Aspiring Directors' programme as an example of innovative and excellent practice.

The Home Office Comes Calling

The Home Office (often referred to as the Department of State in other countries) noticed these two successful projects (and an additional community safety project), and funded Woodward Lewis to build three pilot projects dealing with domestic and gang violence. Jane and her team trained representatives from domestic abuse charities in Blaenau Gwent and Cambridgeshire, and Council staff in a south London Borough. Each group planned a different project but all focused on raising community awareness of violence issues.

In Blaenau Gwent young people were taught to facilitate community meetings, to answer the question "Why does no one talk about domestic violence?" They discovered typical barriers and used PD practices with community members who were able to actively interact with victims. These practices were then used to engage potential victims, encouraging victims to speak about their experiences. Their approach involved convincing pairs of people to talk confidentially, without experts or specialists in the room (but on hand in case of need). Sometimes, sudden and dramatic insights emerged; for example, one mother-daughter pair realised they each were in an abusive relationship. The young people running the project grew in confidence and responsibility. Additionally, according to the local partnership press release, domestic violence reporting in the area increased by 15 percent during the time period.

In Cambridgeshire, two groups were recruited by trained representatives of local charities, one in the affluent south of the county and the other in more deprived, rural north. The southern group consisted of abuse survivors who worked together using PD techniques to discover what enabled them to leave their abusive partners. They created ways of sharing these strategies with other abuse victims. The local head of the multi-agency partnership on domestic abuse was impressed at the way in which PD "de-victimises" people. The PD activity helped individuals move from the limbo faced by many abuse survivors who left their partners who then become dependent on support services. They were able to move on.

In the north, a diverse group with an interest in helping abuse victims were recruited through a campaign focused on rural isolation. They used data and brainstorming meetings to discover the ways that victims without transportation access found ways out of abusive relationships. The group created ways of attracting these individuals to supermarkets and post offices, and subtly offering support such as issuing a coupon with a helpline number hidden in the barcode. (Here too abuse reports spiked, but since official figures are reported county wide, it proved impossible to review the actual data during the relevant time period.)

Lessons Learned in the UK

Jane and her team made several discoveries while implementing and guiding the positive deviance approach in the UK:

- PD's open-minded and positive approach to participants is unusual to front-line staff and vulnerable people. People blossomed, many achieved well beyond expectations, and this in turn made it enjoyable and fulfilling to facilitate.
- It is not easy to get people to focus on and collect data but it provides fascinating insights and helps people to identify the problem (and sometimes people find that the problem is illusory).

- British people generally do not feel comfortable with a self-directed PD approach. Managers in client organisations recognised that PD is a group coaching technique, and that coaching's success and length depends on the coached individual, but they were not prepared to sign up for something potentially open-ended. They needed more direction and structure in the exercises, and this worked well, as long as they observed PD principles. More structure and timescales were required to convince these managers.
- PD can build what a Director-General of the Department of Health called "communities of capability" and can perform "reverse consultancy." Insights and good practices emerge every time.
- Two exercises did not succeed: one community was not convinced that there were problems or that the problems were their responsibility; the second was limited by the behaviour of a manager in a pivotal role and others' fear of her.

Best Use of Positive Deviance

For which types of problems is the use of positive deviance particularly appropriate? Why is PD different?

Horst Rittel, a German mathematician teaching at Berkeley in the 60s and 70s, was one of the first design theorists in America, and he described in some of his early papers what he called "wicked" problems. [8] These problems aren't evil, but rather strange, unusual, puzzling, even intriguing. Rittel and his University of California colleagues encountered issues in urban planning and design. As early as 1964, Professor Rittel outlined his second-generation systems approach during his popular Science and Design seminars, culminating in a 1973 paper written with Melvin Webber:

> The classical systems approach ... is based on the assumption that a planning project can be organised into distinct phases: 'understand the problems', 'gather information,' 'synthesise information and wait for the creative leap,' 'work out solutions' and the like. For wicked problems, however, this type of scheme does not work. One cannot understand the problem without knowing about its context; one cannot meaningfully search for information without the orientation of a solution concept; one cannot first understand, then solve.

To understand wicked problems, one contrasts them with "tame" problems. A tame problem:

- Has a relatively well-defined, stable problem statement;
- Has a definite stopping point, i.e. we know when the solution or a solution is reached;
- Has a solution which can be objectively evaluated as being right or wrong;
- Belongs to a class of similar problems which can be solved in a similar manner; and
- Has solutions which can be tried and abandoned.

Thus, tame problems can be analysed and, further, they can be optimised. Systems thinking and optimisation approaches of linear programming and other management science tools are very effective in dealing with these types of problems.

Wicked problems, however, are difficult to formulate. In Herbert Simon's terms, they are *ill-structured and complex*. Rittel advocated a new approach in dealing with these problems, an approach that takes into account the political and social nature of the environment, as well as behavioural change. PD is an approach that fits nicely into Horst Rittel's view of an advanced systems approach, one that is suited for intractable problems in which the human dimension is salient and requires thoughtful attention.

Today, many approaches and tools help tackle wicked problems, including Appreciative Inquiry along with other asset-based approaches, an entire family of methods that finds and leverages strengths rather than focusing on deficits. The Palo Alto School of Solution Focused Brief Therapy from the psychotherapy field, for instance, shuns older therapies that delve into a patient's history and instead focuses on possibilities and solutions.[9]

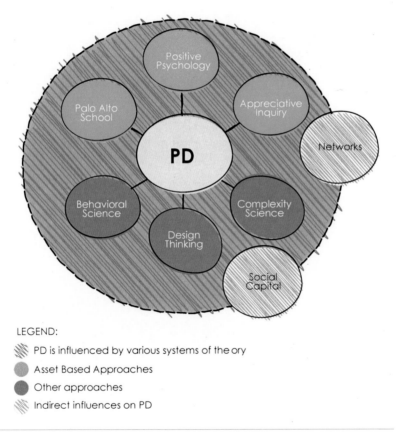

LEGEND:

PD is influenced by various systems of theory

Asset Based Approaches

Other approaches

Indirect influences on PD

Figure 1: A family of approaches

All of these approaches have noble ancestors, among them social constructionism. In books like *Toward Transformation in Social Knowledge*, Ken Gergen advanced the notion that people and societies create their own social reality.[10] While critics attacked a potentially dangerous relativism underlying aspects of his theories, Gergen's intent was to liberate structures and create possibilities for further growth.

Other members of the family tree include several psychologists all working under the rubric of positive psychology, among them Martin Seligman, Barbara Fredrickson, and Rick Snyder. Lastly, other pieces in this mélange of influences are complexity science, activity theory from the world of education, and new findings in brain science and evolutionary biology.

When not to use PD

If your problem is tame, well behaved, or technical, you probably shouldn't use positive deviance.

It is less likely to be effective applied to an environment where top-down or command-and-control structures inhibit employee or citizen empowerment.

Resolving or addressing wicked problems requires an adaptive strategy, and among these asset-based approaches, positive deviance, with its practical "in-the-marketplace" sensibility, has a proven track record over more than twenty years.

From Burma to Boston

After Jerry and Monique Sternin left Save the Children and went from Burma to Boston in 2001 to found the Positive Deviance Initiative, PD began its expansion in the West. With resources from the Ford Foundation, the Sternins set up shop at Tufts University's School of Nutrition. Articles had appeared in *Harvard Business Review* and *Fast Company*, and Richard Pascale mentioned the Sternins in his book on complexity, *Surfing the Edge of Chaos*.[11] Goldman Sachs became an early successful adopter of PD.[12] In efforts to promote PD, the Plexus Institute was a key connector; many early adopters came to PD through Plexus conferences and workshops. Merck and Genentech, among others, tinkered with PD, but PD didn't hit its stride in the US until Pittsburgh's Veterans Administration Hospital experienced an MRSA outbreak.

PD is credited with helping the Veterans Health Administration (VHA) reduce MRSA infections in their hospitals. The original MRSA VA project coordinator, Dr Jon Lloyd, was soon convinced of PD's efficacy in changing the prevailing attitude in American hospitals: that hospital-acquired infections were just a cost of doing business. Hospital administrators realise that basic hygiene and hand-washing effectively combat MRSA, but these actions proved difficult to enforce in American hospitals. This fatalistic attitude came from the US healthcare system's fragmented nature and a culture of "drive through" physicians and entrenched bureaucracies.

The MRSA eradication effort in Pittsburgh was so successful that eventually dozens of hospitals joined the initiative, prompted not only by the VHA but also the Centers for Disease Control. (CDC). Dr. Rajiv Jain at the VHA led the effort that eventually became a nationwide grassroots campaign. Positive Deviance, a bottom-up approach to change, gave sanction to employee creativity. So, education on basic hygiene became part of the process. New procedures were established in diverse hospitals such as to how best dispose of nursing garments or the most effective way to wash bacteria-ridden counters. To date, this has been the single most successful, large-scale PD application in the West.

As PD spread in the US, it was adapted to modern organisational life. For example, in hospitals where schedules are prized and busy professionals cannot meet for hours, short but frequent meetings drive the process. Additionally, at times, hospital personnel found that discovery didn't mean only to discover an existent practice, but sometimes an entirely new way of doing things. In a data-rich environment, you don't *generate* the data, but rather *select* the data best describing the problem.

In 2005, another, more extensive article about positive deviance appeared in the Harvard Business Review[13]. After Jerry Sternin started his stint at Oxford, Jane deployed PD in the public sector in England (see above). Lars Thuesen took PD to Denmark's prison system. Curiously, the only two popular books fully dedicated to PD didn't come out until 2010, two years after Jerry Sternin's death.[14]

The Slow Spread

This timeline capsulises PD's Western spread and, sparse as it is, raises several questions. Why was Goldman Sachs the only unmitigated success story in the private sector? Why was the MRSA initiative so successful? Why has there been so little documentation of the PD phenomenon in literature?

Pascale addressed the issue of limited use of PD in the private sector, stressing structural factors in industry inhibiting the use of approaches like PD.[15] Command-and-control organisations and their power issues straightjacket change agents. Most corporations have tightly coupled linkages, so they can respond to most crises in coordinated fashion.

There are conjectural issues in addition to structural issues. The events of September 11 followed the Internet bust of the 1990s and a series of international crises led to the 2008 recession. The private sector firmly retrenched itself in the US and UK. Companies keen to experiment with new trends and ideas in the 1990s are loath to do so today. These are not optimal conditions in which to build community, and community is both an environment and a value in the PD oeuvre.

Shame plays a major part in the success of the MRSA initiative. Scandinavia virtually wiped out hospital-acquired infections, while 100,000 die from them each year in the US, a serious indictment of the proud and highly advanced US medical system. The empowering nature of the PD approach also plays a part in a fragmented medical system in which protocols are difficult to enforce. In fact, the most flagrant of hygiene violators are physicians themselves.

Lack of PD documentation is more difficult to explain. Perhaps the practitioner-driven nature of PD and its mission-focused perspective causes proponents to see documentation as a burden, simply in the way of saving people or solving problems. If you're truly on a mission, why stop to document or count the victories?

Where Next?

Jane is currently working on a project's first stage, helping up to 50 agencies collaborate and maximise scarce resources to support families with complex needs. Interest is mounting in using PD for staff engagement in emergency services and in improving patient safety in the UK National Health System.

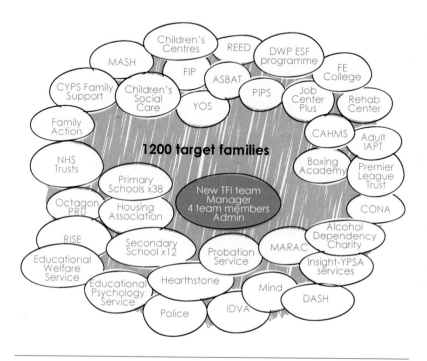

Figure 2: A complex network of stakeholders

Retrenchment, fear, and conservatism mentioned earlier are rife. Managers who do not share the vision and understanding of the leaders who have commissioned the work find it almost impossible to visualise a bottom-up initiative. Yet again, the positive deviants already in the organisation are stepping forward. Will the private sector be a step too far behind?

Roberto is exploring the use of PD as a set of principles, which can inform or guide change management practices within organisations. Collaboration, empowerment, optimism, engagement, communal wisdom, and learning from within, even without a strict methodology, may be a filter through which effective practice is made patent. Good organisations may be those that obtain high performance or those whose employees act in accordance with ethical principles. Better yet, a doubly good organisation, or perhaps a *beautiful* organisation[16], is one in which both high performance and high ethics are the goal. This then becomes an ideal to strive for, much like Keats' "Truth is beauty and beauty is truth."

The Positive Deviance Initiative, Jerry Sternin's legacy, is considering further work in the private sector, targeting community-friendly companies. If one were to ask a "miracle question" – a "what-would-happen-if–all-obstacles-were-magically-removed" inquiry – the answers may point in the direction of highly collaborative, private-public partnerships to amplify positive deviant behaviour.[17] Is it really possible? Only time will tell.

Reflection

Denis Bourgeois and Elizabeth Howard

Denis and Elizabeth were the academic leads and collaborators in founding the CCC programme between HEC Paris and Templeton College, now Saïd Business School, at the University of Oxford. Without them, none of this would have begun.

Many things in life are best understood with hindsight...

When we started the CCC programme ten years ago, we were together in charge of developing an idea that a group of faculty members of HEC Paris and the then Templeton College at Oxford had outlined. We all agreed on basic lines of a content, and more intuitively, on an ethos, on a way to understand our job of executive education. As is often true, we would have had difficulty in describing the ethos precisely. Perhaps, some of it really emerged over time, like the content of the programme, co-created amongst the faculty and the participants.

Most executive education programmes occupy a rather short time span in the lives of their participants. CCC is unusual. Ten years later, alumni of this programme have built a strong group and, among other achievements, have issued this book. Much more than we could have dreamed of at the start, they illustrate what we wanted to convey... and they enable us today to define it more clearly.

We view our job as helping to educate reflective practitioners, that is, people who keep asking themselves questions about what they do: in other words, who do research in their own ways, even if not in conventional academic ways. It also means that they are people who are sensitive and sympathetic to the human aspect of organisational life. Let's say a little more on those two qualities.

Firstly: we have come to the conclusion that we need far more research on intervention in organisations. As academic researchers "We would say that, wouldn't we?" It is not research in the academic world which concerns us here however, but the kind of reflection reported in this book. But if reflection involves reference to theory, going back and forth between data and theory, theory building, constructing action plans based on feedback, data and so on...then it is indeed action research. The ability to carry out research is sometimes described as the ultimate mark of independent learning. Who can doubt the need for continuous learning in our changing environments?

There is too little research on the effectiveness of particular management actions or approaches to change in organisations. Consultant and managers can often be accused of acting irrationally, on the basis of casual benchmarking, or prejudice rather than evidence. Reflective practitioners are very well placed to fill some of the gaps.

We see that change professionals need to be action researchers and perhaps ethnographers in order to work with the realities of specific organisations, rather than ignoring or destroying them in some kind of imposed 'change programme': a more open, exploratory approach to change than many of the 'top-down', formulaic processes that we have seen. This might be described as a humble, or respectful approach to people and organisations and one which we hope we detect in these chapters.

Second, change is trendy; after all, the world itself is changing a lot, isn't it? However, this should not distract change agents from facing two key questions: for which types of changes am I ready to work? Where do I draw the line between ways and means that I feel ethically ok with and those with which I am not? One can see how these issues are present in all papers in this book. In particular, they show how much people can be the solution in change processes whereas they may often be regarded as the problem.

Respecting the human side of change is made possible through approaches where respect for people as human beings replaces instrumentalisation, through coercion or manipulation. These approaches need change agents who have developed their skills in collaborating with human dynamics in social life and in establishing appropriate and respectful interaction processes between stakeholders.

One last word: we have been asked to write these words as we were in charge of the first editions of the CCC programme. However, CCC and this book are collective creations, by their participants and by all faculty colleagues who have been involved. Their beauty is that no one can claim to be their sole author.

We were there to offer a place where people looking for this ethos could grow. Their growth and their learning is theirs. In the uncertain world where we live, it is good news such places are sought.

In Thanks

This book is a project – we kicked it off September 2012 in Oxford. The Change Leaders, as an association, grew out of a master's programme jointly ran by HEC Paris and Saïd Business School at the University of Oxford called an Executive Masters of Science in Consulting and Coaching for Change (CCC). We meet twice a year to continue our learning, share practices and expand our connection with other change practitioners.

Our aim with the 'Book Project' was to produce a useful book for change practitioners in a year. None of us are professional publishers or even writers, although some of us have published books. In project terms, we had a very short (imprecise) goal, no allocated budget and a handful of volunteers. Joanne was nominated as 'leader'.

We began with a simple plan to publish a book in a year. We were told it was impossible, but...

In this process, all sorts of people stepped up and offered help, advice and input.

Our thanks to all those who stepped up enthusiastically with contributions: Chantal Gardner, Joao Steinle, Jane Lewis, Roberto Saco, Lars Thuesen, Mark Munger, Patricia Cichocki, Jane Lewis, Walter McFarland, Susan Goldsworthy, Greg Levis, Richard Coe, Nick Herpers, Mason de Chochor, Marc Porter, Raymond Black, Richard Torseth, Fabienne Munch, Shekhar Pula, Joanne Flinn, Alex Budzier, Daryl Conner, Denis Bourgeois, Phillip Willatt, Mary Akimoto, Jacob Mayne, Margareta Barchan, Jeanne Westervelt

Rice, Ian Read, Hugh McDermott, Dan Ballbach, Steve Johnson, John O'Loan, Pablo Riera, Mike Staresinic, Sharon Wood, Elizabeth Howard, Dorthe Sorensen, Flemming Bentzen, Dennis Vergne, Judith Campbell, Martin Thomas, Silke Grotegut, Anja Reitz, Wulf Schönberg, Mick Yates, and Cécile Demailly.

To those that offered and gave help: Elizabeth Howard, Denis Bourgeois, Rachel Amato, Cécile Demailly, Slim Suleman, Dorthe Sørensen, Philip Willatt, Hugh McDermott and others.

Any community is as strong as its links outside. All sorts of people stepped up to help, particular thanks and appreciation to:

Valerie Sweeney who cast her great eye and good sense over all the articles once we were ready, and to Harriet Morris, Sue Breniman and Byron Nifakis who gave up chunks of August to get us through the final stages with their new eyes.

Our cover and wonderful interior design is due to the creativity and dedication of Julia Beck (who joined our weekly book calls for months before we were ready for aesthetics and marketing), Ghita Benkirane who created the layout and to Cherie Amparo who took on creating a coherent voice in our illustrations.

Rafael Ramirez conceived of CCC, he taught the first module of the CCC programme setting the scene for how the world might change using scenarios. Rafael inspired a vein of thinking towards the future, of considering alternatives, that as change leaders we make very real conscious choices as we step up to lead change. He has been a friend and supporter of our journey – we are honoured in his perspective on change.

Much thanks to Art Kleiner for his thoughtful introduction to change and this book. He inspired us to write at Oxford. We are grateful to pay our respects in our own writing. Art with his deep appreciation and influence over the fields of organisational change and change management is particularly special as he writes from the eyes of the business practitioner

Denis and Elizabeth, thank you. Thank you for creating CCC and thus the Change Leaders. Thank you for crafting a process that changes each of our lives. And thank you for writing the afterword to this book. More thanks!

Of course, the rest of our life supported us. Our thanks to our family and friends who stepped up, provided meals, coffees, companionship and calls to come play when we needed it. Dan thanks Annelle for bringing toast and coffee refills during early morning US time western time zone calls. Mike thanks Nevena, Isaac and Martin for letting him work on the book Sunday mornings. Julia sends a big thank you to Maxi for playing Wii. Roberto forgives his family and friends for thinking he got religion on Sunday mornings. Joanne's appreciates Byron's late night cups of tea and backrubs as calls approached midnight.

Joanne, Roberto, Mike, Dan and Julia

The Book Story

A Change Journey Itself

Now a little on global book projects – we learnt about change. Time changes and conference calls – with people in USA, Germany, France, Denmark, Singapore, Vietnam, Kenya, Mexico, Costa Rica, Nicaragua, Switzerland and the UK depending on travel schedules. Some people were up at 5:00a.m. on winter mornings while others got to bed brains buzzing after midnight when our weekly call finished.

We had our own change journey – we asked the authors to show up – so are doing so ourselves.

As we got underway, we described this project as an emergent project – Joanne manages and advises companies on projects success and project management. She decided standard processes wouldn't work and got agile, time boxing each month to 'what do we need to get done this month' and 'what do we need to prepare for next month'. Then everyone got in and did what they could.

We watched what emerged. We thought we'd get 8-10 articles if we were lucky – we received 26. We thought we'd have funds and marketing support – we didn't. We made choices, not all of which were popular. We kept to the vision – a book, on change, that shows practice and reflection. That shows the practitioner of change. Ready for September 2013.

With our embarrassment of riches, all those articles, we had a challenge – there was no way a group of volunteers who had day jobs, family and other parts of life going on (moving home, changing country, changing jobs, hunting for work, growing businesses, graduations, weddings...yes, life) could get all these into a single book in a year.

We went back to community in Paris April 2013 and put the choice

- A selection of articles that could help each of us in the community to have better conversations about change, or
- One big book, not as tightly conceived, of all articles for September 2013.

The community went for the first. This led to the difficult task of selection. We came up with five criteria and the book team voted. This meant reading all 26 articles – over 100,000 words. Everyone had different opinions! We listed the articles and picked the eight than had the most points on these criteria. Why eight? Simply, so that it was manageable.

We asked each of the authors to show up in their article. We knew each was a master. They had their own stories and scar tissue. Sharing that as well as tools would be a human dimension to the subject of change. This, it turns out, is easier asked than done. One of the team joked 'of course I'm in the picture, I'm the one behind the camera.' Coaching, cajoling and coercing writers that we actually wanted to see them as practitioners turned out to be a change journey of our own. One that we are still on.

We've had a few guiding phrases in our lives as change leaders:

'The race goes not to the swift, nor the most fleet of foot, but to the species most responsive to change' ~ Charles Darwin
- May this book help you and your organisation run your race

'Be the change you wish to be' ~ Gandhi
- May this book inspire you to be everything you can

'Change is a journey, not a station'
- May this book be a useful companion of your journey

As we signed ourselves in our emails to the entire project,

Joanne and the Book Team
the Change Leaders

The Authors

Margareta Barchan, a business strategist specialising in the human side of organisational change is an entrepreneur, consultant and former CEO. She works with companies around the world and serves as a director on several boards. Based in Switzerland and a partner at New Angles, she teaches at leading business schools.

Alex Budzier is researching the role of values and behaviour in executive decision-making and lectures on Project and Programme Management at the Universities of Oxford and Cambridge. He works across Europe and lives in Oxford.

Joanne Flinn is an entrepreneur and change visionary focusing on the human side of success and organisational change. She is the author of the *Success Healthcheck for IT Projects* and a partner at Shelton Consulting. She blends the East and West in work and life, speaking, consulting and teaching globally while living in Asia.

Susan Goldsworthy, an Olympic finalist, passionately combines her experience in sport and business facilitating personal and organisational change. Susan coaches and consults with global clients and at leading business schools. She is co-author of two books; the award-winning *Care to Dare* and *Choosing Change.*

Silke Grotegut is a Human Resources Business Partner (internal HR consultant) for a Bonn-based German firm. Previously she filled various human resources roles, including leadership development, Human Resources strategy and development, organisational development, and transformation management.

Jane Lewis, a partner in Woodward Lewis LLP, supports people to use Positive Deviance with their learning programme, Hidden

Insights®. Jane's 20 years' experience in facilitating improvement in the public and private sectors uses a range of well-known techniques, focusing on the importance of building relationships.

Martin Thomas, the first Chairman of *the Change Leaders*, consults and coaches on change towards sustainable futures. Martin and Mark McElroy currently focus on integrated sustainability performance metrics based on context. His experience embraces four continents and four languages over four decades.

John O'Loan began his career in journalism in his native Australia. He has since been hands-on in most aspects of the media, in most parts of the world. This has given him an exciting front row seat to a dramatic, worldwide change evolution, forced by increasingly rapid technological disruption to the "old order".

Anja Reitz is a Human Resources Business Partner (internal HR consultant) for a Bonn-based German firm. She consulted for many years in organisational and human resources development, change, and transformation management. She also participated in the exciting venture of founding a new enterprise.

Jeanne Westervelt Rice is an executive coach and communications consultant studying the impact of reflective writing on leadership development and implementing system-wide change. She is a partner at Rice + Associates, a New York-area public relations company. She serves as a trustee on several non-profit boards.

Roberto Saco turned a travel hobby into anthropology and then into a global business career spanning three decades. Roberto applies innovative solutions for organisational problems. He is a consultant on strategy and change and an Adjunct Professor in Management at Miami Dade College. He lives in Florida.

Wulf Schönberg is Vice President and Human Resources Business Partner for an exchange-quoted German enterprise based in Bonn. Previously, he was vice president of organisational development and consulted internally and externally for strategic management, leadership, organisation, and human resources.

Mick Yates focuses on leadership development in networked systems, particularly reflecting the impact of Big Data and social media. He is a Visiting Professor at the University of Leeds, a past Board Trustee of Save the Children, and a globally experienced senior executive who has worked across five continents.

Notes

The Road to Redemption, Barchan and Rice

[1] Those interested in the survey and its results can find it at http://www.newangles.eu/2013surveysummary

[2] Klas Mellander, *The Power of Learning: Fostering Employee Growth*, Ontario, Canada, Irwin Professional Publishing, 1993, pp. 10-22.

[3] James W. Pennebaker, *Writing to Heal*, Oakland, CA, New Harbinger Publications, 2004.

[4] Cynthia Roberts, "Developing Future Leaders: The Role of Reflection in the Classroom," *Journal of Leadership Education*, 7, 1, 2008, pp. 116-130

[5] There are many empirical studies demonstrating the benefits of reflective or expressive writing on the immune system, mood changes, and performance, and more anecdotal articles appearing in the media every day. A few samples:

> Kitty Klein and Adriel Boals, "Expressive Writing Can Increase Working Memory Capacity," *Journal of Experimental Psychology*, 130, 3, 2001, pp. 520-533.

> L. M. Barry and G. H. S. Singer, "Reducing maternal psychological distress after the NICU experience through journal writing," *Journal of Early Intervention*, 24, 4, 2001, pp. 287-297. doi:10.1177/105381510102400404

> M. A. Cohn, M. R. Mehl, and J. W. Pennebaker, "Linguistic markers of psychological change surrounding September 11, 2001," *Psychological Science*, 15, 2004, pp. 687-693. An analysis of over 1000 people who wrote online journals in the weeks before and after September 11, 2001.

> Cecelia Capuzzi Simon, "Warrior Voices: Veterans learn to write the words they could not speak," *The New York Times, Education Life*, February 1, 2013.

[6] Kathleen Adams, *Journal to the Self. Twenty-Two Paths to Personal Growth*, New York, Grand Central Publishing, 2004.

[7] Cynthia Roberts, "Developing Future Leaders: The Role of Reflection

in the Classroom," *Journal of Leadership Education*, 7, 1, 2008, pp. 116-130.

8 Cynthia Roberts, "Developing Future Leaders: The Role of Reflection in the Classroom," *Journal of Leadership Education*, 7, 1, 2008, pp. 116-130.

Mobilising Heads, Hearts and Hands, Goldsworthy

1 David Rock, *Your Brain at Work: Strategies for Overcoming Distraction, Regaining Focus, and Working Smarter All Day Long*, New York, Harper Business, 2009.

2 Stephen Jenner, "Benefits Management and the New Science? Author and Chief Examiner of 'Managing Benefits," 2011, http://www.apmg-international.com/en/qualifications/managing-benefits/managing-benefits.aspx.

3 Kurt Lewin, "Frontiers in Group Dynamics, Part 2," *Human Relations*, 1947, pp. 143-153.

4 Stephen Jenner, *Realising Benefits from Government ICT Investment – a fool's errand?* Reading, UK, Academic Publishing, 2011.

5 Donald A. Marchand and Joe Peppard, "Designed to Fail: Why IT Projects Underachieve and What to Do about It." IMD Working Paper [IMD 2008-11] 2008.

6 Peter Drucker, *Management: Tasks, Responsibilities, Practices*, New York, Harper Collins, 1973, pp. 481-492.

7 Reactance: *http://psychologydictionary.org/reactance-theory/*

8 Naomi Eisenberger,"Broken Hearts and Broken Bones: A Neural Perspective on the Similarities between Social and Physical Pain," *Current Directions in Psychological Science*, 21, 1, 2012, pp. 42-47, http://sanlab.psych.ucla.edu/papers_files/Eisenberger(2012)CDPS.pdf.

9 David Rock, *Your Brain at Work: Strategies for Overcoming Distraction, Regaining Focus, and Working Smarter All Day Long*, New York, Harper Business, 2009, p. 27.

10 George Kohlrieser, Susan Goldsworthy, Duncan Coombe, *Care to Dare: Unleashing astonishing potential through Secure Base Leadership*, Hoboken, NJ, Jossey Bass, 2012, p. 95.

11 David Rock, "SCARF: A brain-based model for collaborating with and influencing others," *Neuroleadership Journal*, 1, 2008, p. 2; David Rock, *Your Brain at Work: Strategies for Overcoming*

Distraction, Regaining Focus, and Working Smarter All Day Long,
New York, Harper Business, 2009.

[12] George Kohlrieser, Susan Goldsworthy, Duncan Coombe, *Care to Dare: Unleashing astonishing potential through Secure Base Leadership,* Hoboken, NJ, Jossey Bass, 2012, p. 100.

[13] Matthew Lieberman "Why Symbolic Processing of Affect Can Disrupt Negative Affect: Social Cognitive and Affective Neuroscience Investigations," in *Social Neuroscience: Towards Understanding the Underpinnings of the Social Mind,* Oxford, Oxford University Press, 2011, pp. 188-208.

[14] Stephen Jenner and Susan Goldsworthy, "Realizing Benefits: Winning Hearts & Minds," APMG-International, 2012, http://www.apmg-international.com/en/qualifications/managing-benefits/managing-benefits.aspx.

[15] The Law of the Jungle http://www2.fiu.edu/~milesk/Rudyard_Kipling_Law_of_the_Jungle.ht m

[16] Stephen Jenner and Susan Goldsworthy,"Realizing Benefits: Winning Hearts & Minds," APMG-International, 2012, http://www.apmg-international.com/en/qualifications/managing-benefits/managing-benefits.aspx.

[17] Curtis Sittenfeld, "He's No Fool (But He Plays One inside Companies)," *Fast Company,* November 1998, http://www.fastcompany.com/35777/hes-no-fool-he-plays-one-inside-companies.

[18] http://www.successories.com/iquote/author/190/napoliean-bonaparte-quotes/6

[19] Peter Meyers and Shannon Nix, *As We Speak: How to make your point and have it stick.* New York, Atria Books, 2011, p. 160.

[20] Stephen Jenner and Susan Goldsworthy, "Realizing Benefits: Winning Hearts & Minds," APMG-International, 2012, http://www.apmg-international.com/en/qualifications/managing-benefits/managing-benefits.aspx

[21] Warren Bennis, "Leader as Storyteller," *Harvard Business Review,* January 1996.

[22] Albert Mehrabian, "Professor Albert Mehrabian's communications model," http://www.businessballs.com/mehrabiancommunications.htm.

[23] Daniel Goleman, " Make the Mission Meaningful," *http://www.linkedin.com/today/post/article/20121220212057-*

117825785-make-the-mission-meaningful?trk=eml-mktg-condig-0108-p1.

Performance that Lasts, Thomas

[1.] Globescan & SustainAbility Q1 2013 survey of 1,170 qualified sustainability experts. http://www.sustainability.com/blog/why-unilever-patagonia-and-puma-lead-the-pack-say-sustainability-leaders#.UdR71E1waM8 .

[2.] Robert Cooper, *The Breaking of Nations* , Atlantic Books, 2004.

[3.] Tim Jackson, *Prosperity Without Growth*, Earthscan, 2011.

[4.] Gill Ringland, Oliver Sparrow, and Patricia Lustig, *Beyond Crisis*, Wiley, 2010.

[5.] F.E.Emery and E.L.Trist, *The Causal Texture of Organisational Environments*, 1965.

[6.] John Elkington, *Cannibals with Forks*, Capstone, 1999; *The Zeronauts*, Earthscan, 2012.

TBL: The triple bottom line (... 3BL, and known as "people, planet , profit" ...) captures an expanded spectrum of values and criteria for measuring organisational (and societal) success: economic, social and ecological/environmental." Elkington The Zeronauts p 250.

[7.] Mark McElroy and Jo van Engelen, *Corporate Sustainability Management: The Art and Science of Managing Non-Financial Performance*, Earthscan, 2010.

[8.] R. Edward Freeman, *Stakeholder Theory*, edited by Robert A. Phillips, Edward Elgar Publishing, 2011, p. 230. In addition, "A number of organisations have formal TBL charters, among them the Dow Jones Sustainability Indexes, the Global Reporting Initiative, Novo Nordisk, and SustainAbility. With the ratification of the United Nations and Local Governments for Sustainability (ICLEI) TBL standard for urban and community accounting in 02007, this also became the dominant approach to public-sector full-cost accounting." The Zeronauts p 251.

[9.] Chris Argyris, *Flawed Advice and The Management Trap*, Oxford University Press, 2000. p72.

[10.] Ben Bundock et al., *Digging Deeper*, ClientEarth, 2010. See also public response - Margaret Hodge MP said to the Starbucks' UK

CEO "we are not accusing you of illegal behaviour, but immoral behaviour. You seem to have no understanding of the difference!"

11. International Integrated Reporting Council, Draft Framework, 11 July 2012.

12. Robert Eccles and Michael Krzus, *One Report*, Wiley , 2010.

13. Bill Baue coined the term "thrivance" in 2010.

14. Hardin Tibbs, "The Value Loop," in *The International Handbook on Environmental Technology Management*, edited by Dora Marinova, Edward Elgar, 2006, ch. 35.

15. William McDonough and Michael Braungart, *Cradle to Cradle*, North Point Press, 2002.

16. Bill Smith: AIC, http://www.odii.com/index.php. Accessed 31 July 2013

Organisation 3.0, Grotegut, Reitz, and Schönberg

1 Lynda Gratton, *The Shift*, HarperCollins Publishers, 2011, pp. 23-54.

2 Matthias Horx, "Das Geheimnis der Megatrends," 2010, www.zukunftsinstitut.de/verlag/zukunftsdatenbank_detail.php?nr=2541.

3 Florian Gerster et al., "Arbeitswelt 2030," Friedrich Ebert Stiftung 2008, pp. 7-8.

4 Lynda Gratton, *The Shift*, HarperCollins Publishers, 2011, pp. 34-39.

5 T. J. Mathews and Stephanie J. Ventura, "Birth and Fertility Rates by Educational Attainment, 1994",pp. 20, Monthly Vital Statistics Report

6,8, 10 Jutta Rump, *"Quo Vadis Deutschland?"* White paper, 2009, pp. 3-5. (http://www.ibe-ludwigshafen.de/publikationen/allepublikationen.html)

7 Lynda Gratton, *The Shift*, HarperCollins Publishers, 2011, pp. 30-33.

8 Jutta Rump, "Quo Vadis Deutschland?" White paper, 2009, pp. 7-8.

9 Lynda Gratton, *The Shift*, HarperCollins Publishers, 2011, pp. 27-34.

10 Jutta Rump, "Quo Vadis Deutschland?" White paper, 2009, pp. 8-10.

11 Rüttgers, Jürgen: Zeitenwende, Wendezeiten, Siedlerverlag, 1999. p. 23

[12] Matthias Seitz, "Zur Entwicklung von Wissensgesellschaft und Wissensarbeit," 2006, pp. 1-14, http://www.orientierungsnetzwerk.de/50_kontext/50-01_gesellschaft/pdf/50-01-11_Wissensarbeit_UVP.pdf.

[13] Lynda Gratton, *The Shift*, HarperCollins Publishers, 2011, pp. 39-42.

[14] Florian Gerster et al., "Arbeitswelt 2030," 2008, pp. 9-15.

[15] Jutta Rump, "Quo Vadis Deutschland?" White paper, 2009, pp. 11-13.

[16] Niels Pfäging, "Presenting the BetaCodex. Putting an end to 'command and control': 12 laws for defining the 21st century organisation," BetaCodex Network white papers, paper 06, 2008, p. 3.

[17] Georg Schreyögg, *Organisation: Grundlagen moderner Organisationsgestaltung*, Gabler Verlag, 1999, pp. 130-148.

[18] Georg Schreyögg, *Organisation: Grundlagen moderner Organisationsgestaltung*, Gabler Verlag, 1999, pp. 190-191.

[19] Friedrich Glasl, *Das Unternehmen der Zukunft: Moralische Intuitionen in der Gestaltung von Organisationen*, Verlag Freies gestalten, 1999, pp. 16-21.

[20] O. Branfman and R. A. Beckstrom, *the Starfish and the Spider*, Penguin Group (USA) Inc., 2007, pp. 161-178.

[21] Daniel F. Pinnow, *Unternehmensorganisationen der Zukunft*, Campus Verlag, 2011, pp. 75-76.

[22] Daniel F. Pinnow, *Unternehmensorganisationen der Zukunft*, Campus Verlag, 2011, pp. 88-94.

[23] Daniel F. Pinnow, *Unternehmensorganisationen der Zukunft*, Campus Verlag, 2011, pp. 115-118.

[24] O. Branfman and R. A. Beckstrom, *the Starfish and the Spider*, Penguin Group (USA) Inc., 2007, p. 41.

[25] O. Branfman and R. A. Beckstrom, *ibid*, pp. 59-81.

[26] O. Branfman and R. A. Beckstrom, *ibid*, p.164

[27] O. Branfman and R. A. Beckstrom, *ibid*, p.170

[28] Niels Pfläging, "The 3 Structures of an Organisation," BetaCodex Network white papers, Paper 11, 2011, pp. 5-11.

[29] Ricardo Semler, The Seven –Day Weekend, Arrow Books 2004

[30] Stefan Schyett, Filialen an die Macht, McK Wissen 08, pp. 71-72

31 "Extrinsifier versus Intrinsifier – Interview zu Motivation, Arbeit und Leistung," http://www.lars-vollmer.com/blog/extrinsifier-versus-intrinsifier-%E2%80%93-interview-zu-motivation-arbeit-und-leistung

32 Niels Pfläging, "Special Edition Paper - Turn Your Company Outside-In!, part I+II. A paper on Cell Structure Design," BetaCodex Network white papers, Nos. 8 & 9, 2012, p. 27-29.

Big Data and Leadership, Yates

1 IBM Bringing Big Data to the Enterprise; Analytics: The Real-World use of Big Data, 2012

2 Gualteri, Mike, *The Pragmatic Definition of Big Data*, Forrester, 2012

3 Economist, Big Data: Lessons From The Leaders, Economist Intelligence Unit, 2012

4 CSC, *Big Data Challenges & Opportunities: Empower Your Business With Data.* 2012

5 Hagel, John, *The Power of Pull*, Basic, 2010

6 Siegel, David, *Pull*, Portfolio, 2010

7 Forrester, *How To Engage Your Omnichannel Consumer*, 2012

8 BzzAgent http://www.bzzagent.com/blog/post/colgatepalmolive-pure-clear/

9 Huston, Larry & Sakkab, Neil, Connect and Develop: Inside Procter & Gamble's New Model for Innovation, *HBR*, 2006

10 McLellan, Laura http://my.gartner.com/portal/server.pt?open=512&objID=202&mode=2&PageID=5553&resId=1871515, 2012

11 Lakhani, Karim R. & Lars Bo Jeppesen, http://hbr.org/2007/05/getting-unusual-suspects-to-solve-rd-puzzles/ar/1 2007

12 Economist, *Big Data: Lesson for Leaders*, Economist Intelligence Unit, 2012

13 Keller, Scott & Aiken, Carolyn, *The Inconvenient Truth About Change Management*, McKinsey, 2000.

14 Hanna, Dave, *Designing High Performance Organisations*, Addison Wesley, 1992

15 http://www.kotterinternational.com/our-principles/changesteps/step-1

Straight Lines Won't Get You There, O'Loan

[1] H. G. Wells, Lecture to the *Royal Institution of Great Britain* delivered on Friday November 20th 1936.

[2] Maryanne Wolf, *Proust and the Squid: The Story and Science of the Reading Brain* HarperCollins, August 26th 2008 and other writings

[3] Frances Ongs many writing explore this over several decades

[4] Marshall McLuhan, Excerpts from *Understanding Media, The Extensions of Man, Part I*. Originally published in 1964 with many subsequent printings.

[5] Chris McKenna, Lecture to the *Oxford Business Alumni*, Said Business School, on Saturday 15th September, 2012.

[6] Rupert Murdoch, Lecture delivered at *The London Banqueting Hall*, September 1993.

[7] Don Tapscott, *Crisis of Leadership*, nGenera.com, 2009.

[8] Norman Doidge, *The Brain That Changes Itself: Stories of Personal Triumph from the Frontiers of Brain Science* – Penguin, 2007

[9] Guy Claxton, Wise Up, The Challenge of Lifelong Learning, Bloomsbury, 1999

[10] Maryanne Wolf, *Proust and the Squid: The Story and Science of the Reading Brain* HarperCollins, August 26th 2008.

[11] Jaron Lanier, *You Are Not a Gadget*, Penguin, 2010.

[12] James Boswell, *The Life of Samuel Johnson*, 1820.

Boards Risk It All, Flinn and Budzier

[1] Stephen Bainbridge, "Why a Board, Group Decision Making in Corporate Governance," Vanderbilt Law Review, 55, Jan 2002, p 2-54.

[2] P. Yettonet al., 2003, A model of information systems development project performance. Information Systems ..., 10, pp. 263–289.

[3] Bent Flyvbjerg and Alexander Budzier, "Why your IT project may be riskier than you think," *Harvard Business Review*, Sept 2011.

[4] Chris Sauer, Andrew Gemino & Blaize Horner Reich, "The impact of size and volatility on IT project Performance," *Communications of the ACM* Nov 2007.

[5] Bent Flyvbjerg and Alexander Budzier, "Why your IT project may be riskier than you think," *Harvard Business Review*, Sept 2011.

[6] C. Verhoef, "Quantative IT Portfolio Management," *Science of Computer Programming*, 45, 2002, pp. 1-96.

[7] Joanne Flinn, *The Success Healthcheck for IT Projects - An insiders guide to IT investment and business change*, Wiley, 2010.

[8] IT as a profession and industry measures budget, time and scope, other project types (strategy, culture change, process change, M&A) are less disciplined in this respect but similar patterns are found by those who study it: McKinsey, Bain, Ernst & Young…

[9] Flyvbjerg and Budzier, 2011

[10] J Flinn, 2010

[11] Juliane Teller, Barbra Natalie Unger, Alexander Kock, Hans Georg Gemuden, "Formalisation of project management: The moderating role of project portfolio complexity," *The International Journal of Project Management*, 30, 2012, pp. 596-607.

[12] M. Information, K. Ewusi-Mensah, & Z. Z. H. Przasnyski, "On information systems project abandonment: an exploratory study of organisational practices," *MIS Quarterly*, 15(1), 1991, pp.67–86.

[13] IBM Blog 08/06/16.

[14] Alison Holt, Chair of the IT Governance Working Group, Source: http://www.iso.org/iso/news.htm?refid=Ref1135.

[15] Richard Nolan and F. Warren McFarland, "Information Technology and the Board of Directors," *Harvard Business Review*, Oct 2005; helps Boards assess the strategic impact of IT.

[16] Eveleens and C. Verhoef, "The rise and fall of the Chaos Report Figures," *IIIE*, Dec 17, 2008, P 1-9; highlights the systemic political bias in commonly reported data that makes it look better than it is.

[17] J Flinn, 2010.

[18] B. Flyvbjerg, "Survival of the unfittest: Why the worst infrastructure gets built—and what we can do about it," *Oxford Review of Economic Policy*, 25(3), 2009, pp. 344–367.

[19] David Handcock, *Tame, Messy and Wicked Risk Leadership*, Gower, 2010.
David suggests that Project Management Methods based on process techniques like PRINCE II and PMI and Risk Assessment processes like PRAM, MoR and RAMP are written specifically to deal with simple problems.

[20] Handcock, pp. 51-52 (adapted).

[21] Weidong Xai and Gwanhoo Lee, "Grasping the complexity of IS Development Projects," *Communications of the ACM*, 47 (5), May 2004.

[22] David Dombkins introducing Complex Project Management Standards, Keynote, at the 20th World Congress on Project Management, International Project Management Association (IPMA), Shanghai China, Nov 15-17, 2006.

[23] It's easy to break up a big wicked project into a series of projects that look simple to create a portfolio or programme – it is still a wicked portfolio. This actually increases risks. With individual projects within organisational silos, it's easy for operational levels to overlook risks between projects as interdependencies between projects pay no heed to organisational silos.

[24] Busting the assumption that a portfolio is the simple sum of projects: see Marinuso & Lehtonen 2006, Teller et al 2012, Unger et al 2012, Prifling 2010, Flinn 2010.

[25] For more on what to look for and how to do this, see 'The Success Healthcheck for IT Projects, an Insiders Guild to Managing IT Investment and Business Change' (Wiley 2010)

[26] Heuristics are the scientific term for a rule of thumb.

[27] Paul Goodwin & George Wright, "The limits of forecasting methods in anticipating rare events," *Technological Forecasting & Social Change*, 77, 2010, pp. 355-368.

[28] George Soros, "The crash of 2008 and what it means: the new paradigm for financial markets," *Public Affairs*, New York, 2009.

[29] Gerd Gigerenzer and Wolfgang Gaissmaier "Heuristic Decision Making," *Annual Review of Psychology*, 62, 2011, pp. 451-82. Also refer to Wubben & Wangenheim, 2008.

[30] Gigerenzer and Gaissmaier; Dr Bonman of the International Rice Research Institute (IRRI) at the 50th Anniversary describing approaches to communicating complex science to farmers; G. Klein, "Naturalistic decision making," *Human Factors*, 50(3), 2008, pp. 456-460.

[31] Goodwin & Wright, 2010.

[32] Steve Rayner, "Uncomfortable knowledge: the social construction of ignorance in science and environmental policy discourses," *Economy and Society*, 41 (1), 2012, pp. 107-125.

[33] D. Kahneman, "Maps of bounded rationality: Psychology for behavioral economics," *The American Economic Review*, 93(5), 2003, pp. 1449–1475.

[34] For more on how to do this, see 'The Success Healthcheck for IT Projects, an Insiders Guild to Managing IT Investment and Business Change' (Wiley 2010)

[35] Goodwin & Wright, 2009.

[36] Flinn 2010

[37] Expected yield is used as this links inputs, results and probability of success. Projects with negative yields consume funds, they do not add value. If expected yield is negative, capital is at risk.

[38] E. F. McDonough, & F. C. Spital, "Managing project portfolios," Research Technology Management, 46, 2003, pp. 40–46.

[39] Catherine P Killen and Cai Kjaer, "Understanding project interdependencies: exploring the role of visual representation, culture and process," The International Journal of Project Management, 2012.

[40] Probability of Success less that 1 (100%) represents the discount on ROI/ on a probabilistic basis. In this example, the orange zone is set at 0.4 probability of success. Low odds for a material investment.

Deviance, Discovery and Delight, Lewis and Saco

[1] The Consulting and Coaching for Change (CCC) programme is a post-graduate course offered jointly by the University of Oxford and HEC (Paris) for change practitioners, consultants, coaches, and facilitators. The authors, as well as several others mentioned in the article, are graduates of CCC.

[2] See the following: Richard T. Pascale, Mark Milleman, and Linda Gioja, Surfing the Edge of Chaos, Crown Publishing, 2000; Jerry Sternin, "Practice Positive Deviance for Extraordinary Social and Organisational Change," in Louis Carter, Dave Ulrich, and Marshall Goldsmith (eds) The Change Champion's Field Guide, Best Practice Publications, 2003; Richard T. Pascale, Jerry Sternin, and Monique Sternin, The Power of Positive Deviance, Harvard Business Review Press, 2010.

[3] Sternin 2003, pp. 23-24.

[4] Sternin 2003, p. 28.

[5] Pascale, Sternin, and Sternin, 2010.

6. Keith Ruddle and Jane Lewis (eds), *Exploring Positive Deviance: New Frontiers in Collaborative Challenge*, Saïd Business School, University of Oxford, 2010.

7. A diagonal slice of the organisation takes into account all vertical hierarchical levels and horizontal departmental units. It is an attempt at inclusion.

8. See the following: Horst Rittel, "On the Planning Crisis: Systems Analysis of the First and Second Generations," *Bedriftsokonomen*, 8, 1972, pp. 390-97; Horst Rittel and Melvin Webber, "Dilemmas in a General Theory of Planning," *Policy Sciences* 4, 1973, pp. 155-169.

9. The Palo Alto School of brief therapy, positive psychology, appreciative inquiry, and positive deviance are asset-based approaches. All of the approaches or systems of theory in the diagram, however, have affinities with second-generation approaches, as defined by Rittel.

10. Kenneth J. Gergen, *Towards Transformation in Social Knowledge*, Sage, 1994.

11. See the following: Pascale, Milleman, and Gioja, 2000; David Dorsey, "Positive Deviant," *Fast Company*, 41, 2000, p. 284; Jerry Sternin and Robert Choo, "The Power of Positive Deviancy," *Harvard Business Review*, 14-15, 2000.

12. Pascale, Sternin, and Sternin, 2010.

13. Richard T. Pascale and Jerry Sternin, "Your Company's Secret Change Agents," *Harvard Business Review*, 83, 2005, pp. 73-81.

14. See the following: Pascale, Sternin, and Sternin, 2010; Arvind Singhal, Prucia Buscell, and Curt Lindberg, *Inviting Everyone: Healing Healthcare through Positive Deviance*, Plexus Press, 2010.

15. Pascale, Sternin, and Sternin, 2010, pp. 142-147.

16. We are indebted to Rafael Ramirez at the University of Oxford who opened up this line of inquiry in one of his CCC lectures, although he would probably differ on our interpretation of "beautiful."

17. The "miracle question" is a feature and technique of solution focused brief therapy (SFBT), pioneered at the Mental Research Institute in Palo Alto, California.